Notes from the Road

NOTES FROM THE ROAD

(and the songs I sang there)

Journals, Poems & Lyrics
with illustrations by the author

ELLIS PAUL

BLACK WOLF PRESS

©2002 Ellis Paul

Black Wolf Press
PO Box 381982
Cambridge, MA 02238

Printed in the United States of America

ISBN 0-9720270-0-9

Design:
Sing/Song Books
PO Box 787
New Paltz, NY 12561

To You

"Words are better when they're written down.
They fall to the page
with no sound,
and if you let them sit awhile,
give them time and distance,
you won't hear the rattle in the voice
that gives a fool away
with no choice.
Time is all you have tonight,
so take the time and get this right."

Words, Ellis Paul

Forewords

When I was asked to write something resembling a foreword commenting on my role in this book, I laughed, and I squirmed. Not necessarily in that order. Once I realized there was no wriggling out of it, I asked myself, "What do editors write? What do *I* write?!"

I wanted to be a part of this project because I am an ardent admirer of Ellis' work, and as such, I felt this would give his other fans a glimpse into his creative process—poems and songs that you can't find anywhere else, and familiar things presented in a way you've never seen them before. But the bottom line is that this was fun for me. I hope you get as much enjoyment out of it as I did. Skip around. And go deep...

-Lisa Murdock

I approached Ellis' book like a record producer approaching a batch of songs—ready to trim, tune, highlight hooks, and create harmony out of the cacophony. I had only seen Ellis perform once—for the most part we were strangers to each other.

Yet Ellis handed himself over—although buried in his journals. I intentionally stayed away from his recordings, with their melodies and dynamics already in place, hoping that new songs would emerge. Near the end I began listening to his albums. The words that were so familiar to me on paper now had a voice, as different from their sound on the page as sunlight is from the moon.

I am deeply appreciative of that time where I was the stranger—almost-illicitly intermingling with a few of the intimate thoughts of a soon-to-be friend.

-David Perry

Author's Preface
September 13, 2001

I am writing just days after the tragedy of the terrorist attacks in Pennsylvania, NYC, and Washington DC—the deadline for this book is fast approaching and I have been asked to write a foreword regarding the material included and I can't separate my thoughts on these details from the broader ones of the tragedy. I can't help but think of the backdrop of where I live and how fortunate I am to be here.

I feel very lucky to be able to make music for a living, to write words that people can hear and can read without restraint from government or religion. Our economy gives people the freedom to create, explore and purchase music, literature and art. This country provides a freedom that is present in these ideas and words, and I hope you see the joy I take in writing them.

Initially, I was going to step into a discussion of what poetry vs. lyrics vs. spoken word was here, but it comes down to simply this— these are words and sketches I jotted down in journals, through letters, or lyrics. It's me—occasionally reckless, joyful, somber.

Thank you for opening these pages.

-Ellis Paul

April 10, 2000
Santa Cruz, California
4:11 pm

I am in a wet suit. They call it that for a reason—and it ain't the rain. My Santa Cruz tour guide, Mark, says he's been surfing for twenty years and today I am going to believe him, because trust is important when you're swimming with the sharks. That's where we are—playing with the seals, frolicking with the sea lions, splashing with whatever these wet stuffed animals are that keep bobbing their heads above the water, looking for answers that I can't provide:

"Who *are* you?"

"What are you *doing* here?"

Somewhere in the vast blue deep are dorsal fins and overbites...

Mark is a sandy-haired 40-year-old California wild man who is currently standing on a nine-foot piece of wood coming straight for my head in the wild Pacific Ocean. They call it surfing. For me it is more like falling, swimming, drowning, climbing, and spitting—all in the company of a piece of wood that once was alive, climbable, leafy, with little birdies nesting in it. I've got a yellow one tied to a bungee cord on my right ankle, and Mark lent me his spare wet suit for the day. For me, the water is pleasant, though he's shivering in a two-piece suit, with shorts and a sleeveless shirt. The ocean is a cool 55 degrees and does the sorts of things to the male anatomy that can only be referred to passingly here.

There are about thirty of us out in the water. People are watching from the cliffs up above, and I can't help but think that I used to be one of them. A group of ten or so of us are getting a lesson, and everyone here has varying degrees of skill, me being at the lower end of the scale. Actually, I don't really qualify for the skill scale, but I am at the top of the inept category.

I have been run over twice.

Actually, it feels a lot like Boston traffic. Whoever is moving the fastest has the right-of-way. This means, simply, PEDESTRIANS BEWARE. The first guy to share his board with my head apologized with a French accent. Mark replied for me, "Sorry, about that, man. He's from Boston." The guy said, "Batt, I am frrom Frrawnce," and I know Parisian rotaries—he did have the right-of-way. The next collision was a seventeen-year-old local, Sally, who said, "Sorry," and then swam back to the safety of her sisters. They were all very good surfers, and looked at home in the waters.

My manager would kill me if he knew. I'll call him afterwards, and just drop it in as an aside to my day. Folksinger/surfer…I can hear it now, "No, you might get hurt, you might go mad, you might start saying 'dude' on stage…look where it got Brian Wilson."

However, I am more likely to suffer by my own mistakes than by a wave, another surfer, or a shark, but sharks do cross my mind, even in swimming pools.

I did manage to crouch on a couple of decent waves, but in those two hours among the seals, I failed to become *Homo erectus*. I was just another ape, surfing on my knuckles on a banana-colored board. Mark rode a few waves, looking very comfortable. And he took pictures—me falling, me coming up for air, me mediating international affairs with France, et cetera.

May 7, 2000
Medford, Massachusetts

It is 5:30 am. Birds are chirping; the sun is rising. I have been up all night, the internal clock of the West Coast still ticking inside my body.

The West Coast-me thinks it is 2:30 am, that I am in sweet California just starting to get drowsy. Reality—I am in Boston. The sun is rising. I have a noon meeting; I will stumble into it like a zombie.

I think deeply of songwriting and my work in these obsessive wee morning hours, and I ride a string of ideas like a fantasy magic carpet—one that will lift my life clear of troubles and bring me to a place that will provide answers both spiritually and financially. I am doing music as a Life Choice, for some big pay-off Mecca, and then it hits me. I'm thirty-five and single, relatively obscure, and poor. Then the carpet becomes a train that carries me into some doubtful, uncharted territory of the night.

Everyone has been in this part of the mind before—the "What Am I Doing With My Life?" region. Most of us visit it like a mistaken turn through the seediest part of town, avoiding the sights by looking straight ahead and aiming for the quickest line out.

I am lost in it.

A year ago, my cell phone rang as I was driving down a two-lane highway in North Carolina. It was a friend from Boston calling me with news of the death of a college friend and her family in Mozambique. Barbara Kloeck was 34-years-old, had two kids and a husband, and all of them were killed in a terrible traffic accident where they were stationed doing charity work in Africa.

Technology has amped up the rumor mill; the grapevine is instantaneous. The world is incredibly small. Tragedy happens and we hear all about it almost from the moment of impact. There is no trickle down effect that eases the flow of news, slows the drip of information, or allows us to drink it in at an easy pace.

I am at an age where I know life is fragile, short, and uncertain, and I am thankful for it. It has allowed me the chance to breathe and enjoy time's passing in a way that I could never do in my twenties. I feel like time is an investment now, that it is meant to be spent focused, chosen deliberately, and most importantly, enjoyed. It has made my touring life, performances, and friendships blossom.

The time is now.

People, friends, family—the very things many of us take for granted—these are where our precarious life finds its sense of certainty. We weave this fabric of community to strengthen the fragility of living, to create a sense of sureness, firmness—and to watch the flow of time against each other's progress.

I am traveling around the country, seeing my old college friends who have come to see me perform, and their faces are so similar and yet so different than they were fifteen years ago. We all are collectively coming to terms with ourselves, our own lives, and Barbara's passing.

She could have done anything she wanted with her life. She was truly beautiful, radiant, and bright. She chose the Peace Corps, and we all rolled our twenty-year-old eyes. She didn't seem the mud-hut type, but then she quietly made a life out of it, serving people along with a brilliant husband and together toting their blonde kids around the globe. It was admirable, but she was poor. Their work was the kind that goes mostly unnoticed. Yet she made a big difference for the people she knew and worked with individually, one by one, and *that* stretched across cultures, races, religions—and found its meandering way to me on a deserted two-lane highway in North Carolina, as I pulled over and tried to figure out why the puppet master chooses to pull strings like this.

Occasionally, we are meant to spend time thinking about how we spend time.

A Road Trip in 4 Parts

I

November 4, 1995

59 South, Victoria, Texas

Matt Linde maneuvers through the cow-like traffic that blocks this highway. He requests, occasionally, that I hold the wheel while he dabs at barbecue sauce with his chicken nugget-things. Matt's a filmmaker who is recording a documentary of my tour. I fear having Matt in the car with me in Texas; he sports a Sgt. Rock flat-top cut with lamb-chop sideburns and a foo-man-choo goatee. I suspect that police radar picks up people who enter the state looking like this, and given the long tresses that I wear myself, I know that a visit from State Troopers is in our future.

With this knowledge we have managed to fill the car with the garbage we've collected over the last few weeks—Taco Bell bags from Virginia, a copy of *USA Today* from a Motel 6 in North Carolina, cups and containers and fast-food collectibles from points in-between. Any police searches will have to plow through all this when we hit the obligatory drug stop, and a happy canine sniffs through a carnival of the senses.

It's been a surprisingly great tour so far, with a big show in Boston at the Somerville Theatre, and gigs from Blue Hill, Maine to Atlanta, Georgia at Eddie's Attic and across through New Orleans on Halloween night with ghouls and goblins riding drunk on the street cars, cheerleaders and vampires holding hands in the streets. We just left Houston, where I played to an enthusiastic crowd at the Mucky Duck on a rainy Thursday night. We are bound for Corpus Christi and the Gulf of Mexico, where Matt tells me he will take a pee and thereby mark his territory. It's a big country, but he drinks alot of coffee.

We have had a chance to visit friends and put them in the movie. We stayed with Kristian Bush and Jill Joyner in Decatur, Georgia when we played at Eddie's Attic. After hours Pierce Pettis, Kristian and I played to the wee hours for the staff with owner Eddie Owens fueling us with shots of Basil Haden Bourbon. "Nectar of the Gods, that shit," says Matt, and I would concur with his eloquence.

Eddie was celebrating the recent victory of the Braves in the World Series and I feared I would be only a side note to that celebration, but the room was filled with fans of mine who weren't so interested in David Justice, or Halle Berry for that matter, and I played two shows to a quiet listening crowd. In

New Orleans we stayed with Gina Forsythe and stopped into the Neutral Ground on Halloween night to play a few songs and celebrate the holiday. Gina was dressed as a witch. I went as myself, but nobody noticed. The next day I played "Margaritaville" to six people and a tattooed punk rocker who Matt said laughed at my jokes then whispered "Satan" under his breath. He *must* have gotten them. Shannon Megarity put us up at his mom's place, which was palatial. I lost the rotation for the couch and slept in a room with a grandfather clock that I dubbed Big Ben, as it was chiming every fifteen minutes. We celebrated my two Boston Music Awards with straight shots of whiskey and saw two girls kissing for a photograph at a place with a grunge rock cover band (complete with stunt hair).

II
November 6, 1995
Eunice, New Mexico
11:58 pm

We are hurtling across the planet at 90 mph, a ballistic sagebrush flying across the moonscape that is New Mexico; our only fear now is the occasional armadillo that might be traveling these lonely highways tonight, blocking our progress, if only temporarily. There is a full moon, and Matt is at the wheel like a man possessed, fueled by its gravitational pull and the half-bag of chocolate-covered coffee beans. We just left a house concert in Midland, Texas, a town best known for the little girl who fell down the well. She didn't make it…to the show that is.

Tucson looms in our future, and I am relieved that

Texas is behind us with no visits from State Troopers to report in the captain's log. Fortunately for us, they never caught wind of Matt and his hair.

We broke into another time zone tonight and stole an extra hour for driving. There is not much company on these roads, save for the skeletal rocking of oil drills and the occasional glow of an OZ-like refinery. Matt tells me "Man, this is exactly the kind of place where you could get abducted by aliens," but looking out the window then over to him at the wheel makes me feel like I might already be there. There's no place like home, there's no place like home. Matt's playing some live Coltrane from a gig in New York City, and it matches the hollowness of the land surrounding us.

III
Friday, November 10, 1995
or, 'The Dirty Laundry Talk Show Fiasco'
Motel 6, San Diego, California

Oprah, Geraldo, Ricki, Tempest (I'm cruising the talk show highway)—so much to choose from, so little actually there. This week seems to be make-over time for punk teens and their parents. I've spent the last 24 hours catching up on sleep and day-time television. My laundry is doing loops now at the handy Motel 6 laundromat as I watch *Days of Our Lives* (my laundry was never *this* dirty).

My madcap filmmaker friend has flown the coop for the weekend to attend his brother's wedding in Florida, and it seems suddenly that the world is spinning slower. His caffeine addiction has a way of boosting his hyperactivity to infectious levels, so that I actually have to consume just to keep up my end of the conversation. He's returning shortly, and I'm regrouping here in San Diego, plotting a way to get him on Leeza for a complete make-over when we're in LA.

I played to six people in Tucson on a Tuesday night. I took what is generally known in professional sports as a road beating (the Boston Celtics never had it this bad). But they were six very kind people, and Matt gently reminded me, in his haze, that three were probably executives for Sony—so I better not screw up. I had memories of a night where I played in NYC the day before Thanksgiving to exactly the same number—half of which were VPs from labels. A cockroach traveled across the stage as I played, zig-zagging beneath my feat in search of shade from the spotlight. But, that was then and this is now. I've been sweating out songs in between these talk shows. I got a new one—it's called "My Teen is Pregnant with a Married Man's Baby." It's catchy depending on whether you are ovulating or not…should be finished in nine months or so.

IV
Sunday, November 19, 1995
and/or, 'Big Sur and the Death of the Honda'
I-80 East, Somewhere in Wyoming
8:21 pm

I left San Diego feeling rested and happy to be clear of cheap motel rooms. A quick drive up to LA brought me to my friend Brendan's place, a shack up in Topanga Canyon, where I spent a few days playing the resident beatnik, eating tortillas, sleeping on their couch and occasionally making the snaking drive down to a bar that canyon residents refer to as "Stop & Fight"…though playing pool and pinball were the only actions I witnessed. I played a few LA shows, the most intriguing being a set at the Pasadena Arts Fair, where I got into a volume war with a big band playing a few stages away. Matt, my filmmaker friend, flew in from Florida and met me at the Troubadour in Hollywood, where I was playing with several other acts as part of a "National Academy of Songwriters" showcase. I told Brett Perkins, who was running the show, that no real songwriter would ever use the words "academy" and "songwriter" in the same sentence. "It's an oxymoron," I said, but no real songwriter knows what that means, *really*, including me.

We took the Troubadour's bartender Cynthia out for a Canter's Deli-LA-late-night thing after the show. She was quick with barbs, a well-practiced skill among good bartenders, and she went to slicing up all the wannnabeeees (those who seem to say "Look at me look at me look at me," and then "*What* The *Hell* Are *You* Looking At?!") into tiny minced entrees.

Matt and I left the next morning and I played a relaxing show in Felton, California at the White Raven, and filled the Honda with a case of wine from Jeff Emory's vineyard. Jeff put us up in a home resting among enormous redwoods in the mountains and I briefly forgot my addiction to the concept of motion. I would have stayed put had Big Sur not been calling. You never say "no" when Big Sur calls.

Magnus runs the Henry Miller Library up in Big Sur

and brings in folk singers, poets and artists as a way to keep the Henry Miller blood flowing. He sent Matt and I to the coast to watch the waves crash and the fog roll in and the sunset fall and they all went down simultaneously in a big blurry orange-blue crush. Big Sur is the psychic center of California—all those vibes the rest of the world despises in Californians are bubbling up here. But here, the source is pure, and undeniable. Those epic, back and forth battles waged down in Los Angeles between greed and hope do not exist in Big Sur. The rich and the poor have carved into these cliffs their life dreams, and they're inspiring on every scale.

Magnus and his wife Mary Lu convinced many friends to come into the Henry Miller Library to see me play that night. The twenty or so people made the small room seem larger. Mary Lu lit candles and Magnus served Dixie cups of "Glugg" which is some evil, apple cider-wine-vodka Swedish invention intended to bring on a Prozac-meets-Barry White kind of buzz. It did. Or was it the place? Or Magnus? No one I have ever met lives fuller lives than Magnus and Mary Lu. The cohabitation between artists, cliffs and ocean brings out the best in these people. When Betty Ford opens a clinic to treat the chronically motion addicted, she should build it over-looking these waves and cliffs.

We tore ourselves away from Big Sur to drive to Monterey to play Morgan's Coffeehouse. The Honda was filled with Mary Lu's Big Sur pillows, wine from Santa Cruz, and a few other "otherworldly" collectibles known to come from the area. It was Friday night, and a gentle crowd of Californians showed up in Monterey. I ended this string of shows on a good note, believing the adventure to be finished save for the whir of wheels on the highway. We were now driving, head down, straight towards the East Coast and Boston, Massachusetts. I thouhgt we'd have no stops except for the cheap Motel 6's, 7's, 8's and 9's…I was wrong.

First, let me say that Utah is a great place to total your car. A crowd of people gather quickly. No car passes without inquiry. At its peak, the population on that little piece of highway will be the largest gathering of folks for 40 square miles.

The case of wine strewn in the median caught the eye of the State Trooper, but miraculously even those thrown from the vehicle were intact and corked. Good for us. I was trying to sound as coherent as possible to provide evidence of my sobriety, despite being dizzy and half blind from the whole experience. We had been very lucky. When the car finally stopped, we were both upside down and covered with shattered glass. Matt had been driving, and he got out of the car first and was on my side before I freed myself from the seat belt. Headlights were already stopping, and I could see the silhouettes of suitcases on the grass. The car was totaled, windows smashed, belly-up in the glare of Good Samaritan headlights. Matt was bleeding and laughing. A stress release, I believe, but later he told me that rolling a car was something he had always wanted to do. "This wasn't on my Life Experience Checklist," I told him. "Next time, remind me to avoid you while you are filling out yours."

I was worried about my guitar, which moments earlier had been on top of all the supplies in the back and now was on the bottom. Cameras, film cartridges, batteries, harmonicas, worldly goods and otherwordly goods were littering Utah. And we were hauled off to the hospital before the cops and the wreckers could assess the items, and I worried that some things might not only be broken, but would be missing the next day. Fortunately, this was Utah, and a kind place it is, except for the occasional plastic tarp that blows across the highways and wreaks havoc with out-of-state drivers. Steve, the tow truck guy, said that the State Trooper had ignored the otherworldlies (clearly Utah and Texas are miles apart) and the wine bottles, and we were happy to have met such kind gentlemen while under such duress. God bless those Mormons.

In the ambulance, a bloodied Matt Linde was cared for by two gentlemen EMT volunteers. We were both in plastic neck braces, but I was more concerned about my wallet, which was lost in the wreck in the darkness. So I didn't have it or anything else that could help get us through the next 24 hours. Not that I could see anyway; my glasses were shattered. But one of the EMTs was an optometrist and he promised to fix them the following morning. The other owned a chain of hotels in nearby Evanston, Wyoming. He was kind enough to provide, free of charge, a room at the Weston Plaza Hotel—say hello next time you're through.

Reprinted with permission from
Leak CD Magazine – Issue 9 – Spring '96.
Thanks to Jim Harmon and Lee M. Hurley.

July 21, 2000
Medford, Massachusetts
11:30 pm

Tho' rapid is how my memories go,
I know me and my manager went on the road,
flying down to New York Town,
to talk with a label about selling my sound.
And that's what we did.
We stopped with a skid.
We were whisked to a fifth floor,
led by a kid,
to a fifth-floor-label—RykoDisk—
with Mr. Alago sitting at a table,
spinning my songs, dancing along—
we could work for them,
but don't get me wrong—
it's a waiting game,
and it's always the same—
you see who likes you,
then you see who pays…

So, with a flash of the teeth, I left Michael Alago and the wonderful world of Ryko and headed down Fifth Avenue to meet a producer for my manager's other band, The Push Stars.

The producer is Ric Ocasek, though to call Ric Ocasek just a producer is definitely a serious understatement. I think pop-god is a better title. But, anyway, so, there we were, my manager and me, knocking on the door of the Ocasek brownstone, trying to breathe deeply.

A woman answers the door. We freeze.

Paulina Porizkova. Ric's wife, who we both had to pretend we weren't enamored of. That's who we were hoping it was. But it wasn't. It was the nanny. A cute nanny, but not Paulina. The nanny called Ric, who appeared from the shadows, just like I remembered him from all The Cars videos on MTV—black hair, blue eyes, and the whitest of tans.

He took us downstairs to his basement, which is where he has his studio. We sat there jawing like we were three normal fellas. Well, really, I just kinda kept my trap shut, I was so blown away—I didn't want to look like a nut. But then we said our goodbyes, and he didn't seem to be able to tell.

Who knows whether he'll record The Push Stars— that's up to fate—but me and Ralph were walking down the street hoping that sheer desire could somehow influence the stars. We got in the car and of course some DJ came on and played "My Best Friend's Girl." We just about died from smiling so hard. We never did get to see Paulina—but when Ric waved bye he said, "Been good to see ya."

The next day, at six in the morn, an alarm started ringing. When I woke up, squeezed in a window seat in an airplane, I called the stewardess over. "I hate to have to ask you this, but, where are we going?" She said, "Mr. Paul, we're flying to Alaska."

And we were and we did, and when we landed with a skid, I was driven through Anchorage by a fresh-faced kid to a neon-lit hotel called The Midnight Sun—my Klondike adventure was just begun.

The next day, a folk-singing friend of mine named Carrie and I took to the roads. I was in awe of the sheer amount of lumber. We saw some eagles, an otter, some fishermen and a potter, and I bought some mugs and then headed back to Anchorage.

We drove up to Palmer for songwriting school, just north of Anchorage with a view of the mountains, jagged and snow-capped. We walked to the depot with Dave Van Ronk to meet twenty-seven people who had brought us some songs to work on. Some were quite green, but we like them that way. We created our own little scene there. Dave said it felt just like Greenwich Village, with less black clothing. Four days later at graduation, there were a few Bob Dylans wheezin' away, so we said our goodbyes, did a show down in Anchorage, and then headed back to the States.

I arrived in Boston just in time for the premiere of *Me, Myself & Irene*, and headed to Providence for the party and show, and it was just about the coolest night that I ever had. I saw the movie, heard my song four times, and I felt kinda guilty, like I had dome something illegal. But it was a good crime—kinda like Robin Hood stealing from 21st Century Fox. You should do it some time if you get the chance.

At the party, I got to sing my big song, and the director, Peter Farrelly, said my name, and everybody tinkled their glasses and clapped at their hands. I was a one-man band that night, so everybody had to be quiet, which they did admirably.

While I was toasting Ralph at the party, someone was in the parking garage stealing my cell phone from my car. The whole next week he was answering my messages. I ended up buying the phone back for fifty bucks and an autographed picture signed *"Love, Ellis, GOOD LUCK."*

But before I got the phone back, I did a few more things, including singing the National Anthem at Fenway Park in front of thirty-three thousand Red Sox fans, and some Yankee sympathizers who had snuck into the stands. We won the game 4-2; Nomar hit a double, and the crowd went wild. I took a moment out on the field, bending down and kneeling, scooping up some dirt as a gift to my brother. My brother is a life-long Red Sox fan, and that seemed to make his trip more worthwhile, besides seeing me singing on the big-screen billboard ripping into "The Star Spangled Banner." Thank God I got all the words right.

You'd think with all that something would go wrong, but, no—then Elektra sent us an e-mail saying that they were releasing the movie song as a single. Poet that I am, I said, "Hey! It ain't married, let's let it go mingle! With the Sting songs, the Bruce's, the Whitney's, the Beck's, and I hope it meets one, and I hope that they neck, and run side by side into the radio sunset!"

I packed up my bags for the end of the story, and flew to Oklahoma for a Woody Guthrie festival, in Okemah town, a place with three water towers. Pete Seeger, Arlo, Jackson Browne and I sang Woody songs and acted unruly. We sang songs there with the Red Dirt Rangers, Chuck Brodsky, Joel Rafael and a bunch of others who I didn't know, but became friends with before the weekend was done. I got an Oklahoma tan, and I couldn't help thinking back to ol' Ric Ocasek, white as a ghost.

And that is the story of the best month of my life. Travels and glory and odd woes. I want to thank you for all listening in.

Love, Ellis
Good Luck!

August 23, 2000
Big Sur, California
1:20 am

I think vacation tends to blur calendar dates. I spent the night on top of the ridge talking with Mary Lu and Magnus Toren, my hosts on this wild adventure vacation.

Great stories every night here; hard place to get to, though. It's a long half-hour ride up to the cliffs above the fog line, where mist drifts in all white and blankety around sunset. Great home-cooked meal—squash and pine nuts, green salad, wine—and then the new story of the evening being Mary Lu's run-in with a mountain lion the previous night, hearing heavy footsteps, snarling in the dark, twenty feet away in the blackness.

Later, I am back at the cabin, a twenty-minute snaking-dirt-road drive-at-5-mph away. I am alone in a dark redwood ravine that seems to be the international conference place of white-tailed deer. In other words—a mountain lion banquet hall.

So, with these mountain lion daydreams in my head, I walked down the short drive in the bleak dark, my heart racing, much the same way it did at the beach the first time after I saw the movie *Jaws*. I survived and am writing this as a testament.

Mary Lu survived, too, with the help of a Camel cigarette. She had slipped out to sneak a smoke, and in one of those hairpin ironies where the cigarette actually turns around and saves someone's life, the mountain lion was frightened off by the smokey scent. She was blowing it out vigorously. He didn't recognize it, and figured the fog was getting angry… three soft paw jumps, and he was gone into the night.

Anyway, I am cabin-bound now. Here's what I am working on in the cabin tonight…lyrically.

A song called "The Speed of Trees"—a title birthed from the lips of Lori B, a songwriter friend from San Francisco who visited the cabin here a couple of days ago.

The Speed of Trees

Sometimes
In my bed at night
I'm dreaming that I'm flying
At the speed of light
In two seconds
I'm brushing past
The face of the moon
8 seconds flat
On the surface of Mars
I'm kicking up
The red dust
Drinkin' in bars

I lean back and raise
A toast to the stars tonight

Dreamin' at the speed of light

Somedays,
I'd just settle for
The speed of sound

I'd step off this porch
And blow a kiss to this goddamn town
I'd let off
One of them sonic booms
And break all the windows
In the living rooms
And blow off the hats
Of the boys
At the old fairgrounds

Laughin' at the speed of sound

And You say,
"Go."
Why don't you go then?
If you want to go
Why don't you decide?
Pick a road,
Decide

Is it a train
Or a plane
Or a bride
Decide
Decide
Decide

Your love makes me move at the
Speed of trees
I've laid down some roots
Grown a head full
Of make-believes
But up above me
Where the angels soar
They're rattlin' windows
Blowin' down doors

They look at me here
I'm planted square down
On my knees...

On my knees
On my knees
I'm asking for the speed of trees
The speed
of
trees

October 3, 2000
Oklahoma City, Oklahoma
2:30 am

It's about time. This place has been in shambles, with people stepping over one another in a drunken game of Oklahoma Twister, trying to get to the stage and back for Greg Johnson's annual howl for the ghost of Woody Guthrie at the Blue Door, in Oklahoma City. The place was packed with red dirt accents. I was sucked up into every spoken syllable—like a verbal tornado had come in and carried me off. There is nothing like being an adopted Southerner, and I am so thankful that the Civil War is long over and that these good people have forgiven us enough to allow us to play them our songs, and their songs.

They let us drink their red wine.

Christopher Williams, my band mate, is playing the drums like a man possessed. He left Boston a good Christian boy, and I am now quite sure that the devil spirit of rock-and-roll has infected his drumming feet. He is a'banging the holies right out of the skins and cymbals and they are a'dancing around the room and slipping into the tapping souls of the shoes of unknowing Okeys. This place is a jumping, sweaty, soulful, gospel choir mess…

Don, of course, has always been that way. *No* surprise there. Hell, sometimes I look over and think to myself, "I got the Devil on lead guitar, I got the Devil on lead guitar." On first glance, people here are uncertain about whether he's a neo-Nazi, or Gandhi escaped from Heaven…of course, we know he's Ghandi come home, eating his fruits and veggies, weaving his little yoga dreams.

Austin, Houston, and Oklahoma were the tour's Holy Trinity. These people are nuts—shouting, singing, drinking, happy-clapping nuts. I never saw such behavior in the quiet solemness of Club Passim in Cambridge, Massachusetts, Harvard Square—except maybe on New Year's 2000—even staid New Englanders gotta let 'er rip sometimes.

Last night was a gathering of Woody friends and family. We were singing "This Land is Your Land," "Deportee," "Hard Travelin'" and a million other Woody songs. Lots of standing ovations for the performers; the crowd was mighty gracious to us all, especially the Guthrie family, who came in from Okemah to share in the music.

The place is quiet now. Chris and Don are tucked in, Greg Johnson is trying to sleep next door, and I am still tapping away, wired from a lack of sleep and happy from this wild Southern swing.

Tomorrow we are heading north and giving Greg Johnson his bachelor pad back. Iowa, Kansas and Minnesota—LOOK OUT! We got red dirt on our feet!

We are tracking the Southern gospel cross the state lines...

October 23, 2000
Medford, Massachusetts
10:55 pm

"Check! Checkkkk!" I was singing it, into the micro-phone. The timbre wasn't quite right—"CJ, turn up the high end a bit in the house, will ya please?" The words flew out of my lips and were shot out into the rafters of the Somerville Theater and reverberated cooler, cleaner with the additional dress of treble. Checckkk! Checccckkylsillvokiaaaah! Checksinthemail...

Don was tweaking his backwards electric pedal foot-board. Chris was setting up drums, kicking at them, hitting on them—your normal sound check really, but more activity here tonight, a sound company, light crew, stage managers, caterers, more people, a crowd milling about...

There was no reason to be surprised when I saw her—kids come in here all the time with the crew—but she was standing alone in the box seat that rises up above the right of the stage. It's the best seat in the theater, the kind of seat where you can rattle your jewelry, raise the chain on the spyglass. It's the kind of seat where presidents get shot.

She looked about nine, I guess. It was hard to tell because I was looking up at her, and she could've been taller than I thought she was. She was standing in the box, staring down at me like some green-eyed mechanic eyeing a mint-condition Model T engine ready for disassembly—she was taking me apart nut by bolt. I was afraid she wouldn't reassemble me. She was in an off-white dress. She stood out against the dark of the theater. I thought somehow that her father or mother had taken her, placed her there, and that they were taking in practice, swinging a light on her from across the theater. I couldn't find a parent in the balcony, but the lights were blindingly bright, glaring down on me.

I kept on playing, switching guitars, not staring back mind you, but playing, open C#, open C#, knowing all along that she was watching, and so I broke into an old kid's song that I thought she might recognize.

"Once there was a man who had trouble all
his own; he had a yellow cat that wouldn't
leave his home…"

Looking up at the end of the verse, from the corner of my eye, I saw her bend her head slightly to the side, brown hair falling on one shoulder. She was listening, and I played and played, and when I struck that last chord, "the cat came back, he just wouldn't stay awaaaay..." I looked up at her directly. She smiled—a long, cool, slow one.

"What's your name honey?" I said into the microphone, and out to the theater...

"It's CJ, Ellis—C-J..." It was CJ, coming in all tiny-voiced through my right footside monitor speaker.

"No, man," I said, "I was just asking this girl here, up in the box, what her name was—"

When I looked up, it was all shadow.

Don looked, thinking someone may have shown up that he was expecting.

I said—

"Did you see that girl?"

He was looking at empty aisles—"No." No, he hadn't. I pointed up to the box, but no one saw her, and no one claimed her. No one cared either, and they all returned to their tweaking, their snare-drumming, their veggie-catering.

Before my show, I was in the cold basement of this old place. I had my little ten-by-ten room to warm up in. The place was quiet. Everyone was upstairs for the moment. I could hear Chris' opening set coming down through the floor boards, the squeaking as he shifted his weight from foot to foot. I was tuning, listening, trying to make out the song—

"Ellis."

Nothing…
no one.

"Jesus…" (That was me).

"Ellis."

I felt the cold and damp of instant claustrophobia, and opened the door to see if anyone was in the adjoining room, ruining my solace.

"Hello—?"

The temperature was dropping, fast. I stepped like I was trying to outrun an avalanche to the door across the room, through the opposing door, up, two steps at a time, to the backstage, to stage side, where Christopher was bathed in blue lights and singing. I saw a wedge of faces staring up from the audience.

"Man, are you ok?" It was Don.

I was completely breathless.

"Yeah, I wanted to catch some of his set..."

I sat down and caught my breath, and didn't say a word—still haven't, until now. Neither Chris nor Don know I am writing this.

I watched the rest of Chris' set and tried to forget about the whole thing. I was brought back to the moment, in the theater, with the crowd there, watching. Chris' folks came, and were loving it. I sang his encore with him, and looked up at the box, empty and dark.

During the break, the spotlights went mysteriously off-line. The light crew took forty-five minutes to repair them to the point where they could focus back on the stage, and nobody could explain why they went out. It was going to make for a long night (and it was—thanks for staying).

When I went on stage after the introduction, I plugged in, and my guitar wouldn't play. CJ's tiny voice came through footside, "We should be hearing you..." All my equipment was ready to go. It took a while before I could fig-ure it out, but the fresh battery I had just put in my pre-amp before the show had mysteriously drained. It was brand new—should've been good for sixteen hours. I walked off-stage a little huffed, ran down the stairs and through to the back room to the one last battery, in the little ten-by-ten foot warm-up shack. I bent into the suitcase for the battery, and found it in my hands.

"Ellis."

I'd forgotten about her! I spun around into the dark of the room, it was empty. In my haste running in, I hadn't turned on any lights, and I was using the cracked door of the bathroom light to see around the place. I ran out, FAST.

I ran up the stairs, and only slowed to a walk when I reached stage side. I rolled my eyes to Chris walking in, and Don came over to check on me. I put the battery in, took a breath, and the guitar hit the first sweet notes of "Conversation."

Don's monitor mix was completely askew when we went into the song, as if someone had run to the soundboard and swiped all his knobs with their hand blindly. During the second song, Don's 12-string fell off its stand with a Hendrix-like boom crash distortion. Thankfully the guitar was fine; after a moment of silence, we finished the piece, and stood back from the mikes to regain a little composure.

Chris swore his drum kit was moving all night as he played it. The snare would be three inches off center, he'd hit it again, and there it would go, he'd see it gliding. It was like playing air hockey. The same thing happened with his kick drum, it kept on pulling out, pulling towards the front of the stage. He would pull it back and kick away.

Oddly, the fireplace video we had with us on stage ran out, trickling to blue screen during the last song of the night—and then it turned to live TV! What was happening?

The show was amazing outside of this, really, a sweet celebration, and the best way to end the best tour I've ever had, and I want to thank you all for coming out. But if you know anything about the little girl who haunts the Somerville Theater, let me know.

October 31, 2000
Halloween
Medford, Massachusetts
12 Midnite

I am tucked into my sheets. The wee ghosts and goblins of my neighborhood are finally off the streets, tucked into their own beds, blood streams racing with the sugar and the caffeine of the night's chocolate spoils. It's a good holiday to be around kids, watching them get wound up and then down they fall, crashing into the sheets, into the pillows, into their dreams...

I wanted to share the story of "Conversation with a Ghost" because its background is questioned so frequently, *and* because it is Halloween.

The song is about my old friend Allison Higgins, who passed away from leukemia over ten years ago. Allison gave me my first guitar—she loaned it to me for the summer of my 20th year. She was an incredible person to me.

I pictured her talking to me through the single letters of a Ouija board, spelling out references from our friendship. But the inspiration of the idea was born on a night at Vance Gilbert's Brookline apartment a few years after Allison's death.

Vance and his girlfriend at the time, Margaret, had invited about ten friends to dinner at their place. My girl-friend at the time, Emily, was with me and a few other guests, including a good friend Beth. Vance and I arrived from an outing drinking eggnog. The women were cutting carrots and getting ready for the meal. Margaret was telling an interest-ing story about a Ouija board she purchased at a garage sale earlier in the month for a dollar. When she brought it home she and Beth began experimenting with it, and sure enough, they conjured a spirit by the name of "P-U-G." They had spent the same kind of time on the Ouija board that new-comers on the Internet do on their keyboards. They spent hours laughing and talking—to something.

We decided to pull the board out, Margaret and Beth at each end, guiding the letter triangle. Pug began speaking in alphabet style, and I became the designated question asker, the devil's advocate, the doubting Thomas...

"What is the name of my manager?" I asked. I knew neither of the women at the board would have known this.

"G-E-R-M-A-N-E," it spelled out...

At the time, my manager's name was Sarah Germaine.

We moved on. I thought perhaps one of them might have overheard this.

"What was the name of the last song I played last night?" I asked, knowing neither of the women had been there at the show...

"R-A-I-N," said the board.

The song I had played was called "Let it Rain."

The room was starting to feel smaller.

"What was the drink that Vance and I had at my place before this party?"

The hands, the triangle, roamed across the board, clearly spelling: "N-O-G"...

I ran to the bathroom and locked the door. The board was amazing. I returned nervously.

We then asked the board if Emily's sister was there, and the board responded "yes" and then, when asked if she had a message for Emily, the board responded with "love"... and then we put the board away. This was too much information for the night.

Both Margaret and Beth shared all that they knew about Pug with us—her real name was Margaret Putnam. "Pug" was her nickname. She was a nurse in the Civil War and was married to a Dr. Putnam, who lived on Beacon Street in Boston. She asked that they not go to her gravesite, but told them where it was (I have forgotten the location in the years since). Pug made many predictions that came to fruition including the April pregnancy of Beth, which both women laughed about at the time. Beth ended up having an ectopic pregnancy that nearly killed her a couple months later...

Eventually, they got rid of the Ouija board, and we

all forgot about Pug, for awhile. I wrote both "Conversation" and the hidden track from *Carnival of Voices*, "Ghost," about her. And a couple of years ago, I was playing a gig at a theater in Middleboro, Massachusetts that also doubled as an antiques warehouse. In the green room, where I was warming up, on a shelf at my shoulder, was an ancient directory of Boston for the year 1865. On a whim, I looked under "P" and there it was—"Dr. Putnam," at "675 Beacon Street."

If you listen to the words of "Conversation with a Ghost" you'll hear Allison Higgins' "R-E-S-P-O-N-S-E-S" that only an insider would know, spoken through "letters, sorry so slow, sorry so few…"

Conversation with a Ghost

I'll respond to you in letters.
Sorry so slow, sorry so few.
In a nutshell, I'm much better.
So far the complaints I hear are few.

So how have you been?
Have you been to the races?
Did you take my mother—
is your sister in braces?
I wish I could've been there to see you through.
Hey, are all those things you told me once still true?

Do you remember that time
it was cold in the park?
You were running a race, I was there on a lark.
Who would've thought that New York
could be such a small town...

Margaret is tired,
let's let her get some sleep.
She's bored with these letters,
let her count her sheep.
So goodbye love, goodbye love...

November 20, 2000
Medford, Massachusetts
3 am

The day after Thanksgiving was a cornerstone in my family's house of holiday rituals.

My mother and sisters, in their Women-of-the-House mode, bundled into their winter coats and anxiously prepared the car for a drive down state, three hours, to Bangor, Maine to shop at the wide selection of stores at the Bangor Mall. Lit up in the white breath of winter, four of the Paul clan stepped into the car with a little bag of cookies, water for the drive, and blankets should the car go off the road and they be stranded in a snow bank waiting for a tow, all dressed in orange, so that they wouldn't be shot by hunters on the way down.

The roads would be filled with automobiles from the County making the same journey down, families out doing that first bit of Christmas shopping. It was likely that if they got into trouble, someone they knew would stop to help. The community made the threat of black ice feel tolerable out on the Maine highway.

My Father and I would leave the new found solace of the house as well, get into the truck, and drive fourteen miles to Washburn, Maine to my Grandfather's potato farm, one hundred and forty acres of forest and fields. We would park the truck roadside and head to the woods in search of the perfect Christmas tree. My father would carry the chainsaw; he was always particular about his trees. His choice would invariably be the top half of a twenty footer, sometimes fir, sometimes pine, and he would lean into that with branches cracking, the chainsaw roaring, and him screaming some pleasantries if it was slow going.

The top half would eventually lean, then fall crackling through the brush, sending up a cloud of displaced snow as it landed on the ground.

What looked like a tree would be a cowering bush by the time we had hauled it through the snow that mile or so back to the truck for the ride home. It was heavy labor; sometimes we would bring a giant piece of cardboard to act as a sled for dragging the tree back to the truck. It was one of those times that can seem really quite romantic in hindsight, out there in the woods, deer running about, finding and cutting down the perfect tree. But in the moment, you are cold and wet, sweating, and cursing your own memory for painting the experience as one that should be repeated annually.

My father would smile over at me when we finally were back in the cab of the truck, he'd start whistling "Christmas, O' Tannenbaum" for fourteen miles, long and chirping through the streets of Presque Isle. He wouldn't start up the barrage of curses till he attempted to get the damn tree out of the truck and through the damn front door of the house, leaving a trail of needles and sap stretching from our living room behind him, out to the truck, and out fainter still down that road winding all the whistle-way back to Washburn, Maine.

Getting the tree into the red base stand (a medieval torture device) was an act combining pure mathematical genius with the brute finesse of a caveman. My father whittled down the trunk of the tree to fit the base, then tightened and stripped the screws bare with vice grips into the tree. Then together we'd count to three and hoist it up into the corner of the living room, where it would stand momentarily drunk as if waiting for the sobriety test to commence.

Annually, the trees seemed to prefer to lean rather than stand upright in their base, but eventually my father would place a nail in the wall on each side of them and wire them into a military stance befitting the honor of their role in the holiday. Then he'd stand back and take a good long look at that tree. He'd be whistling "Silent Night," and he'd witness the gaps in the fullness of the tree, where branches were missing, had been broken, or were simply sparse.

(It was odd—it was as if he was looking at himself in the mirror, like he was contemplating hair loss...)

Then, he'd take out his drill and he'd bore holes into the trunk of that poor tree and then stick spare branches into the holes to fill it out until it was stuffed and fully green, fat like the turkey on Christmas day. He'd then trim the tree as a whole, kind of like a shrub gets clipped in the summer, and he'd even the sides, moving around it like Michelangelo. Then lastly, he'd cut off the very tip-top branch for the star, which would often lean off-center as well, until it was secured with various wirings into a perfectly symmetrical stance. We'd gather and *"ooh"*...

It ended up something of a Frankenstein-looking thing. Which leads me to a thought: why buy an artificial tree, when you can make one yourself at home?

The finishing touches would be perfected, the women would return around nine, flushed with the excitement of the crowds at the mall and whispering about the secrets of their shopping bags, and my father and I would play coy, like the tree had appeared all on its own, like it had managed to spring up through the floorboards of the house to announce the coming of Christmas day.

Then we would gather to fight over tinsel placement.

Holiday Song

I'll be home for the holidays.
Just 6 months and look, here's snow.
I'll speak truth on Christmas Day.
I'm still missing you.

Born again,
Are angels laughing?
Probably, at me.
I've switched my holidays.
Me and timing always seem to disagree.

It's a long road up to Maine.
This highway never changes,
Just me…
Just me.

December 6, 2000
Medford, Massachusetts
11:50 pm

My heat is cranked to seventy tonight, because I feel a bit of December creeping in through the cracks around my windowpane. I like that part of living in the Northeast, when you are tucked in your blankets and comforters and you can feel some tiny frigid jet stream that has somehow made it down from Canada into your apartment, drifting up and across your bed, exploring the corners of your face, blowing your hair back off your forehead. It's a little like camping indoors.

My street is exceptionally lit up this season, providing a beacon of light to the jets taking off from Logan Airport. People drive from miles around to be temporarily blinded by the decorations here. I imagine astronauts can see Wareham Street from where they work above us on the space station.

I live in an Italian neighborhood in Medford. In the summer, I awake to the ladies next door screaming at each other in a flood of English and Italian curses. It gives an Old World flavor to my day. They are a mother-daughter team, and their dialogue is punctuated by those easy one-syllable, reliable English language f-words that we all use occasionally. They are sealed in tightly for the winter now, and I don't hear much from them unless one of my friends accidentally parks in their driveway. The rest of the street is pretty quiet— a middle-class neighborhood where kids run around and play and everyone is friendly. People know me by name and we all treat each other with a distant kindness.

Seventy percent of the houses on my street have a Mary-in-a-half-shell, and now, of course, with the Manger scenes comes another Mary, Mary II, the glow-in-the-dark Mary, Mary and family—like Carnival cruise ships trying to out-do themselves with improved models. The houses have the illuminated baby Jesus surrounded by Joe and Mary and the three wise men, with the half-shell Mary and her special guest, Frosty, peering in from the side. It must have been a cool night in Bethlehem. I've heard Frosty generally avoids the desert. Rudolph is nearby as well, mechanically bobbing his head, hoping to get a little hay from the donkey and the camels in the side-stall.

Two houses down, the strobing brightness of the twinkling lights is enough to send epileptics into seizures. Someone should paste a giant Surgeon General's Warning on the premises. I noticed that the family turns off the yard after ten o'clock or so, when the kids are off to sleep, to save themselves some money and to create darkness for the chirping birds who have been completely thrown off their daily cycle.

My street has become a target for slow-driving tourist types. I think these are the same people you might find leaf-peeping in the fall in Vermont. They have decided to turn south and find the streets of Boston that are most likely to cause power outages. I was behind a parade of three cars that stopped in front of the house today. They were frozen in place—kids in the back of a station wagon completely mesmerized. I must admit, it's cheaper than Disney and nearly as overwhelming. I sort of expected that they would be piping out "Jingle Bells" through their living room sound system, but they are not. I think their power is on the verge of breaking a gasket. The entire city dims when they turn on the yard at five o'clock. I would try to get a picture, but their place is an international religious shrine, both for the States and for Italy, and it probably shouldn't be photographed, especially with a flash bulb.

The neighborhood truly brings out an abundance of cheer, and the kids love it, which makes me love it, and I can poke fun of it at the same time. It makes me remember that I am growing old steadily. We all are, and sometimes I need to be reminded of what a kid's perspective of the universe is.

I do miss Maine and Christmas at home—snow provided the environment where a single candle in a window would bring on that wave of warm, holiday melancholy. There is no snow here, and there may not be any this season, but Christmas happens regardless of snow.

No matter how contrived
　　　　and over-the-top we get
　　　　　　with the ads and the gifts
　　　　　　　　and the decorations,

this calendar season—
　　　　without calling out
　　　　　　the obvious religious overtones—

makes us take notice
　　　　of who and where
　　　　　　and what we are—
　　　　　　　　and of what we have.

This moment is a real gift,
　　　　no matter how gratifying
　　　　　　or difficult it is
　　　　　　　　to be in.

We all collectively contemplate
　　　　our own private versions
　　　　　　of "what was,"
　　　　　　　　"what is,"
　　　　　　　　　　and
　　　　　　　　　　　　"what could be."

It's the only holiday that causes
this three-fold piece
of self-awareness:

Reflection
On your Past,
Acknowledgement
Of the Gifts
In the Present,
And the Hope
That the Future
Will be Better
For All of Us.

December 13, 2000
Medford, Massachusetts
8:30 pm

Over the weekend, the anniversary of John Lennon's murder passed, and I performed a couple of his songs at my shows here in New England and had the crowd singing along. Everyone knew the words. There must be Beatles' DNA strands in all of us.

At the Rock and Roll Hall of Fame, his bloody glasses and his bullet-ridden clothes are on display in a glass case, where people weep in front of it. Yoko wanted the violence of his murder to be on display for the public, in part to help keep his murderer behind bars. It seems that public opinion is with her, and he'll stay there despite efforts for his parole. So far, so good.

Lennon was the three-dimensional Beatle—the comedian, the angry one, the sensitive one. Paul's rock songs, brilliant as they were, were attempts to one-up John, and they scored big frequently. He is brilliant as well, but Lennon was my favorite. There was a desperation in every one of his songs, every note, every word—a need to express his anger, a need for love, a need for humor and a need for compassion. These were the cornerstones of every one of his songs.

Lennon *had* to be heard, you can't keep a man like that down. I've been listening to him myself lately; the John and Yoko interviews with *Playboy* magazine in the Seventies are now out as a book, and as a companion volume there's a collection of great interviews from *Rolling Stone*.

John took his role as artist/ambassador for peace very seriously, which nearly got him deported, and filled CIA files with useless shit about his day-to-day activities.

I wish he were around to comment on the current state of affairs. Wouldn't that be fun! Maybe he could report from the front of the White House, covering the Bush and Gore election fiasco for the BBC. I'm sure he would've cut through the haze with some sarcastic bright-white insight.

There are artists out there—you can see the John Lennon in them. I love these people—Ani DiFranco, Rage Against the Machine, U2, REM—the artists that are writing about the world that *could* be.

Buy their records, and give them to your niece for Christmas! Lennon's legacy is brought wider and wider by their successes.

Who Killed John Lennon?

Do not mention his name.
The man kills John Lennon, now he's on TV again.
He's blaming Holden Caulfield in the face of the lense,
And each time he does it, he kills him again.
Who killed John Lennon?

A loser with a pistol, a martyr's best friend,
And each time he's televised, he kills him again.
It's the prize that he wanted when he loaded the gun,
And each time he's mentioned, murder is done.
So, who killed John Lennon?
A no one.

He's on TV again. He's playing the hero.
The networks won't let the story end.
He brings in the ratings for them.
He's playing the hero, but he's a killer,
He's been convicted.

His lawyer must think it's a game,
Though he knows Lennon's songs, both in word and by name.
He cold calls the networks, retrieves all the funds,
Then he scrapes his percentage when the programs are run.
Who killed John Lennon?

A lawyer, an agent, big money's best friend,
And each time he's televised, they kill him again.
It's the prize that they wanted when he emptied the gun,
And each time he's mentioned, murder is done.

January 27, 2001
Boston, Massachusetts
9:45 pm

On the way home from Indiana yesterday, the rent-a-car bus driver was inquiring whether I was a musician. I guess the guitars were a dead give away. We got into talking about writing songs, and how long they take, and where the inspiration comes from. I told her that sometimes I write the songs, sometimes they write themselves, sometimes the rhymes write 'em. It all depends on the inspiration level, and how much I get out of the way when they come rolling through.

Most of the time I feel like I'm holding onto a hose that is connected to some geyser of inspired word-picture-stories that splash on the page.

There is something insane about it. You have to be partially unconscious to let the words flow freely without putting too much thinking into the mix. You think and "write" in the aftermath, editing phases, trying to make sense of what you've spilled on the paper.

The underground collective subconscious is something we all have in common. All of our collective stories and emotions and histories exist there. This is why I don't feel like I am the source of the songs, but more the medium for their arrival in the conscious world. It gives you more objectivity when looking at them, and though you feel less responsible, you feel no less proud. Well, it isn't my fault I wrote that! It must've come from somewhere in the collective unconscious—blame it on the masses.

So yes, I am working now, and writing. A few songs are being hashed out. Here's one. Chris is the kid in the book *Into the Wild* by John Krakauer, a true story of Chris' travels around the country hitch-hiking, walking, looking for some internal peace...

The Ballad of Chris McCandless

We met on the highway.
He was smilin',
A mystic in torn blue jeans.
The kid left his trust fund to come out walking.
He said, "I'm Alexander, Supertramp,
A Star catcher, a Chaser of dreams…"
I could've sworn he heard the earth a'talkin',
talkin'…

"Sometimes," he said, "don't it feel
like the concrete's closing in?
We're putting bricks on the horizon…"
Was he chasing fool's gold,
Or a holy man walking
a dirt road till the end?
I don't know but
I hitched a ride with Chris McCandless.
I stepped in the wild of a dream.

The horizon in South Dakota
was an ocean of harvest grain.
In a dusty silo we found work for the taking.
We'd hitched up from California,
But he never told me his real name.
Never told me what past he was out here shaking.
We're all shaking something.

"Sometimes," he said, "don't it feel
like technology's closing in?
We're raising towers on the horizon…"
Was he chasing fool's gold
Or a holy man walking
A dirt road till the end?
I hitched a ride with Chris McCandless
I stepped in the wild of a dream—

a stone,
a path,
a river of glass,

The night sky—
Hey, can you see stars
From wherever you are?

With both feet on the planet
Can you feel this old world
Spinning around you?
The pull of the magnet
Is gonna take you from your town,
Your home town.

In a broken school bus they found him
In the heart of the Alaska range
The journey ends
When the heart stops beating—
Our time is so fleeting

Sometimes, don't it feel
like the concrete's closing in—
like we're putting bricks on the horizon?
Are you chasin fool's gold,
Or a holy man walking a dirt road
till the end?
I don't know, but
I hitched a ride with Chris McCandless,
I stepped in the wild with Chris McCandless,
And I felt alive with Chris McCandless.
I was wide awake in the dream,
the dream,
the dream.

January 30, 2001
Medford, Massachusetts
10 pm

     This was a ten-minute timed writing exercise I did tonight. I do these every once in awhile, usually with partners who assign the topics. The poem "Harmony" from the live album was my reading of a timed writing exercise used to introduce Patty Griffin at the Somerville Theater a couple of years ago. I think they can show you how your mind works on its train of thought, and they can often produce a line or two to create something else, like a song, or at least a piece of one.

     Take one phrase, or a word from below, and use that as a topic springboard for yourself. If you're interested in trying it, write for ten minutes (don't cheat) then stop and clean up the punctuation and spelling.

FRIENDSHIP...

all creatures crave the comfort of the cave, the companion-
ship of co-owning friendship, these wild escapades bring wild
blind charades, two man parades, jungle tirades, hand in
hand, woman-woman, man to man, chip me away for the
who that I am, carve me like you would a friend, whittle me
for the shit I'm in, clean me like a bedside maid...

laugh with me, laugh at me, cry with me, cry for me, change
me by asking that I change, be there, be gone, but never too
long, we ripen much sweeter with age...

share my page, co-write my words, our lyrics, our songs entwined and then heard, at least by us, it's a pretty small bus, but we'll invite some hitchhikers along...

ride with me, abide with me, hasten me, chasing me, chastising and chiding me, safely survey the bride for me, approve her and the ring for me, and love me when I've turned to "we"...dress up and fess up and puff out your chest for me, fight for me, knife from me the oh-too-sweet scent from me...carry me, pray for me, tarry the day for me, hoist up a glass, lets drink to the last of we, never let pass the opportunity to celebrate our unity...

February 5, 2001
Medford, Massachusetts
10 am

I was traveling last week and stayed at a bed and break-
fast called the La Vista, built in 1837. I used the setting as a point
of reference for a writing exercise. The ground rules are simple.
Pick an object, small or large and give it a voice, give it a person-
ality. I spent half an hour on this.

La Vista Plantation
I was raised up brick by brick by black hands in the
year of our Lord, 1837, in Fredricksburg, Virginia by 30
slaves and a handful of white men working for plantation
owner Edward Jenkins. He hammered a sign at the end of
the carriage road leading up to my steps—"La Vista
Plantation." But Massahs the only one who can read the sign.
I've seen alot in my day, 165 years of days, one come after
another till here we are. The new Missus, current Missus, she

got me turned into a fancy bed and breakfast, all history books and puffy little pillows. She been serving white people wheat toast and eggs, just like the slaves that used to grease the pans downstairs in my kitchen.

There were over 100 of them working this plantation till that day in 1864 when an army of blue come marching across the fields, down my carriage path, up my steps. The Missus Jenkins, she come screaming into my kitchen, yelling "Bury the silver! Take what you can carry and go! Hide in the woods!" But the men in blue took all she had, and all Fredricksburg had, and 10,000 lives, and left the ground red and grey and blue.

Most of the slaves went with the Yankees, and they left me hollow. A few stayed on, some of them whispering they had it better before Freedom come from the North. "We poorer now," they say. Ain't nothing for free but freedom, and really, freedom had its price. Nobody was giving them clothes, and giving flour, salt—nothing free no more. The plantation was stripped down to sharecropping and that's just slavery with poor man's money and a white man's thank you. But the whippings stopped, and some of them former slaves started in reading, voting—for a while at least—and I could hear them in the basement kitchen, cooking and talking about their husbands' choices above the fire in the stove, "We could send a black man to Congress!" Then I saw a band of white hoods come 'cross the carriage path, with torches and horses, years after the war, shaking at the sky with rifles, and shouting, "Keep them nigger voters at home."

The current Missus found a picture of me at some

flea market from 1857, with Missus Jenkins looking out from my balcony, along with kitchen slaves—Edna on the right on the stairs, Georgia (she's the little one), and a few of the others. Some say it was the first photograph ever taken in this state of any one building.

I loved Missus Jenkins, and she loved me. She treated everybody well. She was almost a slave herself to me, to this home, these slaves, her man. He didn't want her reading nothin' but the Bible—and only goin' to church and nothin' more. He and his poker friends, rich plantation men come here some weekends talking over cards and whiskey glasses in the parlor. "My woman stays home. She runs my home, she runs my home slaves, she runs my children, and she run to church on Sunday." They were afraid of what they were hearing about the Northern women, city women, organizing, fighting slavery, fighting to vote. Missus Jenkins, she was tied to me like a ball and chain. She had the company of her three children and slaves, but that weren't much company.

Nowadays, there's a trickle of white people sleeping in my rooms, making love, making speeches, whisperin' about ghosts runnin' the halls. There ain't no ghost but me. My pipes crack and groan at night and wake up these folk in their 'antique' beds—hell, *antique*, they ain't fifty yet!

No tobacco, no plantation, no slaves, nothin' but a trickle of tourists and an herb garden out back. But, life is good, I'm well taken care of, and treated like a museum in the eyes of those who come visit. Maybe I'll see you sometime signing my guest book, eating toast and eggs at my table come morning in the kitchen.

March 23, 2001
Medford, Massachusetts
9:45 am

I have finally, gladly, emerged from a month-long sabbatical of song writing and meandering through the streets of Washington DC. What an amazing city! I had told myself I would do this for a long time, and I managed to finally put it all together. I explored the city, wrote, and edited songs. It was a working vacation, and I feel refreshed and ready to dive in again. These kind of vacations generally never work out this way, but luck and will-power were on my side this trip. Special thanks go out to the Schementi's who helped me set up a furnished apartment at Randolph Towers in Arlington for the month, my home away from home.

A bit of a concrete jungle is being built there in Arlington, but the conveniences of city life have never been more present for me than in that block near the Metro—movies, coffee, bookstores, restaurants—all at the base of my building.

The highlight of the tourist part of my visit was going to Ford's Theater in DC, where Abraham Lincoln was shot. The blood is still visible on the clothes he wore that evening. The gun—a little Derringer—that was in Booth's hand that night is there, as well as the hoods worn by the conspirators on the day of their hangings. There is still a level of tension in that building, and awe, and grieving. He was a great man, and I believe our world would have been a much better place had he lived in it longer, to guide reconstruction in the South and to help ease the newly freed slaves into their new society.

Most people don't know that Booth didn't act alone that night in April, 1865. He and a band of conspirators were out to assassinate almost the entire Lincoln Cabinet.

General Grant was supposed to be at the theater that evening with Lincoln, but he begged out of the engagement because Mrs. Grant so disliked Mrs. Lincoln. Major Rathbone attended with his fiancee, Clara Harris, instead, and he suffered a serious knife wound from Booth in the process. Booth had intended on doing the same to Grant that night, and he had even visited the hotel of Vice President Andrew Johnson before attending to the theater to do him in as well.

Secretary of State Seward was ill in bed with a metal

neck brace to help him with the whiplash he suffered from a recent carriage accident on the same evening. He was attacked by one of the Booth conspirators, a man named Lewis Powell, who broke through his home, stabbing Seward's son, then running like a madman into the Secretary's bedroom, and stabbing Seward repeatedly along the face and neck, only to have the knife deflected by the metal neck brace. Then, he tore down the stairs and into the night. Seward's jugular vein was saved from the knife by the brace, though he was scarred horribly, and thereafter, he chose to pose for photographers only in profile, showing his unblemished side.

Four of the conspirators were hung within a matter of days, including Powell. Booth was found in a barn in Virginia, and he died from a bullet wound that occurred during his capture.

Booth was a very famous actor at the time and had free access to Ford's theater to set up his crime. He was a bit of an egomaniac, a womanizer, and a drinker—not necessarily in that order. He wanted to be a hero, though most people, even Southerners, were tired of the fighting and looked at peace as a relief. Because of this, the nation as a whole, including a great many Southerners, saw him as a lunatic or a coward for his actions.

A friend and I had a great meal at a place called Sequoia's, which was a wee bit pricey, but if you have a vacation, you should spend at least one night living like a rock star. A bottle of wine, Shafer merlot, 1997, was amazing and pretty expensive, though it is probably around thirty dollars or so if you can find it in a store. It was one of the best wines I have ever had. The place sits along side the Potomac, and we walked from the steps of the Capitol Building, down the mall, past Lincoln's Memorial, past the Kennedy Center with a full, bright, golden moon rising above the monuments and the trees. I will never forget that night, nor the walk, and the meal was an amazing payoff. The wine took away the chill from the evening.

Another highlight of the past few weeks was finishing some new songs. Here's a finished one. This story is a composite of real stories meshed and blended from my high school years.

Eighteen

It was a summer night
I took off in my father's car
I rolled the windows right on down
I cranked up the radio
And chased the meteors
Down a dirt road out of town

Tonight
There's a party out in Walker's field
Tonight
By the firelight our dreams revealed
Tonight
Turn your back upon your high school years
Shadows dancing wildly at the scene
But I never knew right then
Just what it means
To be eighteen
To be eighteen

The voice of Jimmy Aberdeen
Still washes over me
He had a laugh like a thunder cloud
He held a can of blue spray paint
Jimmy was no saint
But he knew how to draw a crowd

That night
We climbed the water tower in Walker's field
That night
Above the lights of town our fates were sealed
That night
Jimmy fell down through the darkness

An ambulance brought silence to the scene

And carried off the life
And broken dreams
Of Jimmy Aberdeen

Now ten years have passed
The cabbie taps the glass
We're in front of
My high school's reunion hall
He leaves me to the night
I count the satellites
I see the tower
Looming tall...

Tonight
I'm taking on my memory
Tonight
I climbed the water tower, so the town could see
Tonight

I painted steel
With cobalt blue
Spelling out
Our graduation year
Above the highway
That took me out of here
And I finally think
I really know
Just what it means
To be eighteen
To be eighteen

August 20, 1995
Hollywood, California
2:30 am

Bobby Leversen is sitting with his back to the blue of the Pacific Ocean. A cell phone is in his hands. He's talking fast.

"Chris? This is Bobby—I need a crew for tonight for a shoot in Malibu. Two cameras. Lights. Can you call Gary and see if he's available?"

Bobby is a mover. A shaker. A Hollywood player. The first of his kind that I ever met. In his fifties, he's living the lifestyle of some character from a Don Johnson TV series. He's rich. He loves women. He parties. Not necessarily in that order.

Bobby made his fortune in the Sixties and Seventies working for Proctor and Gamble developing ideas as broad as the mood ring and Pringles potato chips. I have no idea what the connection between these products may be, but I'd venture to guess marijuana was involved. He currently runs an on-line gambling business. And he's marketing a sexually provocative answering machine tape. He somehow manages to be quite charming despite all this.

"Bobby—listen."

That's the voice of Ralph—Bobby's friend, my manager—who is trying to intercede on my behalf. Bobby has just learned about a radio interview of mine tonight and is lit up with possibilities—a film crew, lights, TV placement. It's a human interest story and would be great publicity. Our mistake was telling him about Brian May in the first place.

Just down the road from our swank eatery, Brian May had made a home for himself on a cliff overlooking the Pacific Ocean. He was the host of a syndicated radio show called *Malibu Folk*. (Who knew those two words could coexist side by side?) The program went out to about 80 radio stations around the country.

Brian was a paraplegic. When he was five years old, he was vaccinated with the rest of America's children in the 1950s for polio. His batch of the vaccine was flawed, somehow, and gave him and a group of kids the disease out right, rather than preventing it. He received a government pension for his troubles and had outlived everyone's expectations, and most of the other victims of the program. He had a house, sound gear, and a passionate life focused around music.

Music took him places that his physical limitations could not. His show was heard across the country, from Oregon to Massachusetts. It raised his spirits and his love of life.

Ralph and I eventually managed to get Bobby to come along for the ride. No cameras, no lights. An elderly woman answered the door. Brian was behind her in the living room, being rolled into position by his assistant (who we later learned was his wife, the elderly woman was his mother in-law). He was sitting upright inside a box on the end of a small bed on wheels. The box was covered in a white blanket with only Brian's head showing. He had an oxygen tube coming out of the base of his neck that disappeared into the box.

"Come in guys! Good to see you!" His eyes were positvely lit up.

We said our "hellos" as I sat down in a chair in his living room behind two microphones. The wall next to me was made up of racks and racks of recording equipment. Brian spoke quietly to his wife in Spanish, directing her movements, placing the earphones, tweaking the recording equipment, adjusting the microphones. She was serving as his hands.

The interview was over in 45 minutes. It was one of the best interviews I've ever had. Brian knew every one of my songs. He was quoting lyrics and talking about connecting themes between them and albums as a whole. It was a conversation with someone who had studied my work into the wee hours—reading lyrics, dissecting the instrumentation, pouring over the credits for the musicians. I had almost forgotten that Bobby was in the room. He sat in the corner wide-eyed, behind Ralph. Quiet. I could tell he was amazed. Brian had had a heart attack in the week prior to our visit. He told Bobby and Ralph that as the paramedic was lifting him into the ambulance, he got upset at the thought of missing this Ellis interview. Music was his mission.

In light of all this, it's easy to see the human interest side of the story—the struggle for Brian, overcoming limitations. The victories were obvious, but the mystery was his attitude—you couldn't help but be amazed by it. He didn't come across like he was struggling, carrying fear, doubt or a false sense of over-confidence. He wasn't a prize fighter trying to conquer an opponent. We can gripe about the smallest things in our lives. God knows I do it all the time. I got the feeling that Brian May was happy. Happier than almost all of us. And I have no idea how he made that happen.

We said our goodbyes and walked on the beach in Malibu. Bobby remained pretty quiet for most of the night. In hindsight he knew the film crew wasn't appropriate for the interview. He was soaking it in. Later on at a beach club in Malibu, we drank with the owner of the place, telling our stories. The owner was in mover/shaker mode as well, dropping names of famous producers and record label friends who stop by to drink scotch at his place. Ralph and I played dumb and, surprisingly, so did Bobby.

Bobby turned the conversation towards a story of when he was a kid, going to Yankee Stadium for a game. He was thirteen. He ended up sitting next to Marilyn Monroe and Joe DiMaggio in the stands. Marilyn, who was not much of a baseball fan, took little Bobby under her wing for three hours, bought him a soda and walked around the stadium with him. It was a day he never forgot. He's been addicted to the buzz of celebrity ever since. It brought him to Hollywood and to the entertainment business.

It hit me—how these singular moments can guide the entire course of a lifetime. Brian got the polio shot. Bobby got Marilyn.

I scrolled back to a few moments of my own thirty years, searching for the one that might have guided me here to Malibu with Ralph and Bobby, watching the waves roll.

May 25, 2001
Machiasport, Maine
11:40 pm

I am sitting in the crow's nest of my father and mother's place in Machiasport, ME—Maine. The night is breathing cold darkness against the windows, and I can see no lights out on the ocean. All is blackness outside, but the lights are bathing me in yellow. My friend Sharon is scratching at a journal, my parents have stepped off to bed, and the crickets are playing Mozart. A winding road through the thickest forest in the northeast brought us here. Finally, after five and a half hours of driving, the bright blue view of the ocean broke across my windshield, and there was quiet calm.

I am still writing songs in my head, in my car, in my living room, preparing for the next session of recording, and the plans are constantly shifting, with producers and labels still up in the air. What kind of record? A folk record? A rock record? A folk-rock record? A rock-folk-polka record?

The drive was all about thinking, deciding, lyric changes, et cetera. I love drives for this. I listened to Bob Dylan's *Live from Albert Hall 1965*—an audience member shouts "Judas!" at him for performing rock music that night. Dylan called him a liar, and screamed at The Band, "Play fucking loud!" You wouldn't think this much history could be captured on a wee little tape; it was evolution happening out-loud—the moment the folk-rock cocoon burst wide open.

I often think people pigeon-hole their favorite artists into a comfortable box, and while some artists seem too eager to stay there, doing the same album over and over again (sometimes successfully), some can't stand to stand still.

Then there are people like Neil Young, U2, Joni Mitchell, Dylan, REM, and Madonna who keep shape shifting, and you just try your best to keep up.

I am beginning to trust that my path will stray and re-align and that forward progress is continuous—though never in a straight line, it's never crazy.

I love doing music, but I may never have a straight answer about its continued success for me; that's the beauty of the unknown. Tonight, I pondered just being a painter—I was looking at Winslow Homer's watercolors—and the idea of standing still or writing books and short stories for a living. Looking out at an ocean can do horrible things to your sense of pace. Your joints start rusting on the spot; you want to build the farm house, plant the garden, mow the yard, feed the chickens.

I can do music *and* these other things, and there's plenty of time to enjoy the spaces in between as well—life happens in the nooks and crannies.

Land is cheap here—$200,000 can buy you multiple acres and rooms with a view. I could only get a one-room condo for that in Boston. Funny world…

Find your ocean, lake, stream, or shower and breathe.

September 22, 2001
Medford, Massachusetts
8:15 pm

The roads up in Maine were alive with cars and pick-
ups headed to and from the turkey festivities. Some carried a
deer as a hood ornament. I am settled back at home now, at
my desk, with turnips and boiled onions dancing in my belly.

Was I thankful on this Thanksgiving Day? I looked
across the table at my friends and family, and thought out
loud about it with them. This year, more then ever in my life-
time, I am more aware of the fragility of life. I recognize my
luck in having my health and heart in a good place. I ran my
eyes across them all with a prayer for protection, guidance,
and dreams fulfilled.

It hit me, as I was sitting with my fork and spoon in my fists, what a bizarre grouping of people we were, gathered under the guise of *relations*. I thought to myself—if there wasn't a blood and family connection, none of us would be here, eating this meal together. My family members are so very different from one another—it's comical that we sprang from the same loins.

The differences in personalities, jobs, income levels, political leanings—all of it—struck me as incredible. Why aren't we more alike? It's amazing to me that we get along at all. Don't get me wrong, I love the differences, too. I can always count on perfectly opposing perspectives from everyone. A family gathering is a great way to learn about the broadness and multiplicity of human world views, if you are into that kind of thing. We sometimes call them loggerheads during the holidays.

I don't look much like my parents. My father is 5'-10" and has been around 220lbs most of his life, and my mother is about 5'-6". They both have blue eyes, though. They are politically conservative, and neither of them were outwardly musical or artistic as adults. Actually, I am glad they know as little as they do about the wild path I have been taking. When I told my parents that I would be a musician, and after it became clear I was serious, taking it out of the *hobby zone,* they were reluctant to offer support.

I can't blame them for this, especially now, having seen the ups and downs of the road that took me here. It looked much easier ahead then it does behind me, though it has been an incredibly rewarding road. I remember my father giving me the graduate school speech, about how I couldn't do music for a living, that it wouldn't be fruitful financially.

He was right! I may never be rich, but my income is now larger than my parents' income was while I was growing up. They are now very supportive of what I am doing because it doesn't seem so risky. I was thrilled to have them at the Thanksgiving show in Maine. I could see them in the crowd, their gray heads swaying, in time no less! There was a sigh of relief afterwards, from both sides. I watched my father sing in a barbershop quartet at a small church in Maine the next day—like son, like father?! And this time, *he* was the nervous one. I gave him the ole graduate school speech afterwards for good measure.

I have a brother who is a lawyer. He's very different from me in many ways, but at least he looks like me. He lives in Denver. And he thinks and speaks in conversation like you would expect a lawyer to think and speak. I believe that doing any job over time infuses you with the personality of the job itself. I am a songwriter; I have been for fifteen years, and because of this, I speak in metaphors that come flowing into conversations like rivers of information (see!). And my jokes are often rhyming word-plays or spontaneous songs that pertain to the moment in some songwriterly way. My brother's jokes are often legal observations, but he's still funny. We see the world from vantage points that are miles apart—we share 25% of the same genes, and none of the same perspective! I *love* that my most likely potential organ donor is a lawyer. But actually his perspective is more valuable to me because it *is* different than mine. He informs my view in a way that I couldn't myself. Is there some Darwinian connection to the survival of families because of this? Will someone's DNA be more likely to survive because it gets a broad range of free opinions from the characters in a family? Do families with twins suffer from a lack of diversity?

My brother's view:

"Remember this—no matter who they are—no partner is too good for a pre-nuptual agreement."

My view:

"Trust your instinct."

My sister is married to a lobsterman on the coast of Maine and has four kids. She sees the world through the eyes of a mother, and I love her observations because of this. She seems to be able to break down the moment to its essence immediately. She would've been a great counselor—except, of course, for the fact that, like any mother, she tells you directly what she thinks rather then trying to lead you there quietly on your own. "Let's cut to the chase, you're single, you're 36, and you're not married." It's often that kind of thing. Her views come without bullshit. She didn't have time to play around and raise four kids that way. She had to get to the point with four of them at the same time.

And her kids are as varied as their aunts and uncles— a flamboyant NYC art student, a very quiet, large Maine mechanic, a highschool cheerleader, and a bubbly clown five-year-old. There's more to them than this, of course, but you get the picture—broadly divergent people under the same roof, from the same blood.

My other two sisters are both Christians and live

within the culture of Christian life. They are active in their church. One is a musician (in grad school, no less). The other is a housewife and has her kids enrolled in a Christian day-school, living in the suburbs in a gated community, comfortably blending in with a bunch of other suburbanites. They are also a great source of wisdom to me because they are so different from me.

What I am trying to get to here is realizing, outloud, the confounded strangeness that I may have more in common personally with Vance Gilbert, a black man raised in the city of Philadelphia and a great friend of mine, than I do with my own family. Though he is from a different part of the world, a different income class, a different race, a different education, and different DNA, I can finish his sentences and predict to you right now—with a great deal of accuracy—what he is doing in the heart of his home at this very hour—gluing a wooden model airplane together—and how he may feel about the death penalty, or herb gardens. We think alike, feel emotions the same way, laugh at the same jokes, even tell the same joke (though he's louder about it than I am).

That is what is amazing to me—the family tree is born of sturdy, diverging roots. I love my family; they are good people. I am the only folk singer in the group. The one they are most often wondering, "Where the hell is he?" Let's hope your family only has one as well.

April 2, 2002
New York, New York
4:30 pm

I'm on West 57th Street in New York flipping through the pages of Woody Guthrie's life. Ralph and I are at the Woody Guthrie Archives. Nora Guthrie, Woody's daughter, is sitting at her desk in the adjacent room. She's smiling at me through a head of curls.

"Find anything interesting yet?"

"Did you know that Woody wrote 'Swimmy, Swim, Swim' for you?"

"No!" she said, "How do you know?"

"He wrote 'For Nora' in the upper right hand of the lyric sheet."

Nora rose from her desk smiling, came in, and leaned over the typewritten page.

"That's what I love about searching the files—you find something new about Woody every time."

I am here searching for a lyric that has survived without music through the last four decades. Nora has asked me to scour the files so I can put the words to one of these songs to my music. Anyone who knows me knows that this is my equivalent of co-writing with Jesus Christ.

Woody died from Huntington's Chorea after a long hospital stay in the Sixties, when Nora was very young, so she had very little time with him. She calls him "Woody" during our conversation rather than "Dad." Her understanding of him has come from family, friends, and the massive archives here and at the Library of Congress in Washington, DC.

Woody wrote constantly—letters, poems, stories, songs. He sketched as well. By the end of his life, he had written a handful of books, drawn thousands of sketches, written thousands of songs, sent thousands of letters—all on yellowed paper, napkins, paper bags. I am sitting here at 37 wondering what the hell I've been up to the last twenty years.

A friend of mine once asked me, "5,000 songs!? Were any of them good?" They were all Woody songs. Priceless. Picasso took to paying bills with a doodle and his signature, knowing that the value of that scrap was worth more than a T-bone steak at a restaurant. A Picasso doodle was "a Picasso." Each had his fingerprint. I feel the same way about Woody's work. Some of it was done while he was sick, hastily written. You can tell his state of consciousness by the quality of the handwriting. But each one is a Woody Guthrie moment, a thought, a breath. Priceless.

Ralph sits across from me smiling. We are wearing white gloves to protect the papers, manuscripts and doodles.

The files smell of Woody's Coney Island sweat. His creative mind was insatiable. Constant. It's hard to not be amazed by the volume. Here are the original lyrics to "This Land is Your Land" with a different title—"God Blessed America for Me." It has been called one of the greatest songs of the Twentieth Century. I came across "Hard Travelin'," "Deportee" and many more of his famous pieces—it was like bumping into old friends at the train station.

We found eight potential pieces, most notably "Be Good to this Boy on the Road," a story of love on the road, and "God's Promise," written when Woody was trying to keep his faith together in the hospital. Felicia, the on-site anthropologist, will research each song and see if they are indeed Woody's and check on whether there is published music for them. I hope to include one of them on my next recording. I'm crossing fingers, toes, and hairs.

I am lucky to have found Woody.

There are all kinds of songwriters you can be— punky, angry, poppy, syrupy, political, analytical, cynical, criminal. The approach doesn't matter. Honesty does.

He taught me to write what I see, and to lay the truth between the lines, so people come to it on their own. My backbone as an artist gets aligned by spending time with Woody. If you are curious about this phenomenon, you can see the ol' Guthrie chiropractitioner yourself inside the pages of Joe Klein's great biography, *Woody Guthrie, A Life*. Or come down to the archives and meet Woody yourself, and give Nora a kiss for me.

June 2, 2001
Medford, Massachsetts
10:05 pm

I walked in Davis Square here in Somerville and the place was filled with people. Summer came knocking loudly at our doors tonight, and people stepped out to see who was there.

The warm breeze on their faces is billowing shirts and skirts. I am free tonight, and I haven't been around on a Saturday in what seems like many months. I forget what this night looks like from this side of the stage, because I am always performing somewhere. It's funny how days of the week have characteristics—how Monday is so slow, Friday so thankful, Sunday so laid back. They sound like the Seven

Dwarves!

Happy is Friday, of course, unless you are unemployed.

Dopey would have to be Saturday night—the drugs, alcohol, your state of mind.

Sleepy—Sunday, until noon if you're lucky, or a musician.

Grumpy—definitely Monday.

Sneezy—Tuesday, when the cold kicks in from the weekend kill of the immune system.

Doc—Wednesday, taking vitamins and drugs to fend off the cold that you created by said weekend system killing.

Bashful—Thursday you have to ask the girl/guy what his/her weekend plans are.

You get the picture—or Disney does.

I've been hanging out with a musician friend who has a couple of babies and still hasn't played music in his life at the level of success he wanted, and I can see it's eating him up, especially recently. The mid-thirties will do that to you. I keep telling him that it is never too late to start; and he's already got the chops and I think he would like to play more, but he is looking for an easy way to break into playing. It isn't easy. It is a combination of luck, talent, work, faith, and perseverance. It's just like any other job that elevates the soul of the person involved.

I think it is never too late, but with kids tugging at your sleeve, the distractions and financial limitations are pretty obvious. But someone once said that trying only takes time, regret stays with you forever. So, I hope he goes for it.

His kids may appreciate his efforts if he follows the course of his dream, whatever it may be. The list of life's late bloomers is enormous—Henry Miller, Van Gogh, Shawn Colvin, Don Conoscenti! Who knows when someone might bloom; it's all about the act of blooming, not the "when" of the bloom.

So bloom…

Take the photo…

Write the poem…

Kiss the girl…

It is never "never…"

It is never "too late…" The only *never* axiom of truth is "never know till you try."

I might be a commercial fisherman before my life is over if the right impulse catches my heart.

Poems

Last Call Poem

Last call gets called out across the length of the bar,
And I tap my pockets for the keys to my car.
I'm wondering if the hotel is too far
To risk getting caught in the glare of blue lights.
And the waitress comes over like I'm her long lost friend,
And though the liquid hasn't seen bottom, she fills me up again.
She's mixing the drinks and the messages she sends,
So the tip jar gets heavy tonight.

In the back room, I see a woman check the angles on the eight.
The crack of a match tells her cigarette's fate.
And before she pockets the ball,
She raises her eyes to her mate
And I turn my eyes to avoid the view.
    I'm not blue, it ain't just blue, it's a deeper, darker hue.
    It's red for the passion, it's green 'cause it's new,
    It's yellow for the coward who's thinking of you.
I left the hotel room to get the phone out of sight.
It burned holes in my retinas from being stared at all night.
And I can't say I'm sorry 'cause you won't allow me to fight.
I'm wrong and there's no place to put the confession.

The jukebox quarters, they go straight to John Prine,
So I can't seem to tear you from my mind.
You're etched in each and every passing line,
So regret buys the drinks not forgetting.
    I'm not blue, it ain't just blue,
    It's a deeper, darker hue.
    It's red for the passion,
    It's green cause it's new,
    It's yellow for the coward
    Who's thinking of you.

Mr. Parks

Mr. Parks
went outside
with no pants
on

his brain
had died
finally
from
a lifetime of thinking

but the sun
felt good

the air
was clean

at the police
station
they asked him
for identification

"It's in my pants,"
he said

his daughter, when
called, was in the middle of an
inopportune moment
with a diaper in mid-change

"Could you call the nursing home?"

At the nursing home
the so-called assisted living center

an impatient receptionist
referred them to the son

Mr. Parks, Jr.

Junior was in a board meeting
and therefore unavailable
referring the call back to his secretary
who then
called his wife

Mrs. Parks, Jr.

who
wondered when dialing
the police station
why she was asked at all
as a family member
once removed

but that was their common bond
she thought
as she grabbed her keys
for the ride
to the station

You Are My Sadness

Look how I carry you
In my eyes
In my shoulders
My walk
Each step
One further
From shelter

Look how I carry you
In my voice, my mind
In unkind dreams
That remember
You are my sadness

I once carried you
Light as pride
You lifted my voice
My step
My spirit
And now
Carved by this weight
This absence
Look how I carry you

Love's Too Familiar a Word

I stepped into the room late last night,
because late is the time I keep.
You were sleeping warm as coal
in a pocket of comfort and white sheets.
But you don't startle anymore when I step into the room,
though the hour is later than midnight,
and neither window can place a moon.
"I missed you," you say,
and it sounds like a promise
when whispered half-asleep,
your skin still damp with sweat
from thoughts your dreams refused to keep.
I follow my memory to a switch on a light.
"Shut your eyes," my voice cut short
when darkness turns bright.
"Do you love me?" you say,
but love is too familiar a word,
for in this bed, 10,000 times it's a phrase already heard.
But, "Yes, I love you," speaks my reply,
though I know I failed
myself and you
for not matching how I feel
with higher words.
I know it must be lonely in the world tonight,
because there's more here than what's deserved,
and the imbalance can't be summed in black and white
because love's too familiar a word.

She Wasn't Listening

Van Gogh took part of him,
carved through the bone,
the skin,
the cartilage,
to give to her a piece of him,
a gift for her,
a piece of him,
because she wasn't listening—
she wasn't listening.

Though his art could speak
in speeches, speak
with every stroke,
his colors spoke
in brilliant rhymes,
chromatic lines,
but she wasn't listening—
she wasn't listening.

She said,
"Vincent Van Gogh,
your learning curve's slow;
you paint sunflower tragedies,
star-light calamities,
you feel your love
like a malady.
I'm looking for a melody…"
But she wasn't listening,
she wasn't listening.

Man, Looking for Kind Woman

It said simply, "Man, looking for kind woman."
And thousands applied, thinking, "Here's a kind man…"
His message read, "Send photo." And they did.
He threw out 2,713 pictures.
To 312 he sent a joke about a penguin.
Those who laughed wrote back, so to 37,
He sent a photograph of a woman compromised.
6 answered with intrigue, 31 with disgust
And from the 6 intrigued he asked
For recipes.

A souffle,
An omelet,
An angel food cake,
An almond salmon surprise—
All appeared in his mailbox the next day.
(2 did not reply)

To the salmon dish he wrote—
"Will you marry me?"

"Will you love me?" she responded.
He hadn't thought of that…
"What is Love?" he returned.
"Love," she wrote, "forgives unkindnesses,
Renders beauty transparent, knows sex is shared,
Endures salmon and salmonella,
And knows philosophy, because it is one."
"Oh," he replied, "I wasn't thinking…"
She wrote again, for the last time—
"Honey, you are far too kind."

Harmony

Togetherness
Discord
Sweet fifths and scales
of Peter, Paul, and Mary
Simon Garfunkel
Cake with layers
Chocolate fudge
Piled up one on top of another
Icicles of high-pitched Bee Gees
Hanging from the house
CSN, folky males, warm tones
Nash screaming for that one high note
no man with both testicles could hit
And hanging...
Hanging...
Hanging
about to explode
courage in musical form
Barry White grumbling like a boiler down on the lower end
gravel is on the bottom
a bumpy slow ride
hot warm southern notes
Billowing like a curtain on an open window
Beatles
Playful male voices
with white guys
Mop tops

Singing like the girls
The Sharelles, the Four Tops
The Mormon Tabernacle wall of harmony
Thick rich chocolate cake so thickly stacked you can't take
more than 5 minutes
One 3 5 7 9th chords and minor 5ths
Dishes stacked and stacked
Harmonization
Why can't we all get along?
Movement in parallel lines and textures
Of 2 voices 2 perspectives 2 minds
Sonny and Cher, James and Carly, Ian and Sylvia
Me and Patty
Her voice torn in the right place
Mine smooth and high—soft
Working like a wool blanket on a cotton sheet

Road Bound

We are road bound, we're chasing the sea
Pretty Girl in the front seat
and she's wrapped around me
You slept through Virginia
woke up in Tennessee
in a sleepy old town
on some old battleground
We put up our tent
as the town clock rang three

A statue woke the morning with the fog rolling in
a general on a stone horse
the champion of men
But I'm glad I'm through fighting
the wars I can't win
and the fights I can't lose
I'm gonna pick as I choose

We packed a one-way suitcase with a map and a jack
We burned all the bridges
and we're not turning back
And if they all come looking
we'll lie about the facts
from an Arkansas phone
to the folks back home

We're Road Bound, gonna swim in the sea
Touch the blue waters, let them crash over me
When we reach California
we'll fall to our knees
The Angels and palms
are singing Beach Boys songs

Be
for Sadie, 3-11-00

Be Careful, be Wild
Be Old, be a Child
Be Grounded, be Light
Be *Certain*

Drink wine from a glass
or a bottle that's passed
Sing songs
Until your throat starts hurtin'

Love hard, Love soft
on the beach, the hayloft
get sand in your toes
it's Christmas

Every day is the Gift
that closes the rift
between the Now
and the sweet reminiscences

Tornado Girl

Sandy has seen a tornado
more times than she's seen the Grateful Dead...
She lives in Oklahoma,
where the storms come prairie fed,
and the numbers keep on mounting.
It's been twenty times now and counting
that she's been in the path
of splintered trees and twisted lead
That connect the dots between trailer parks
with destruction that's painted blood red.

And now she wants to chase them,
with *ME*, in my Honda Civic,
"We'll keep a safe distance."
I say, "Give me an instance
where 'safety' is *MILEAGE SPECIFIC*..."
Okemah is where the last one touched down,
(that's Woody Guthrie's old home town)
and (as if it would turn me around)
she starts singing "This Land Is Your Land."
I say, "OK, you win...terrific."

Now, I've never been to see something
that I wished wasn't even there,
Though I've heard that said of dentists,
and with in-laws, and from victims of the electric chair.
But there I was, heading east on 44,
getting pelted by hailstones
the size of barn doors
So, of course, *NONE* of them were missing...
It was as if *GOD* was keeping score,
and the heavens were thundering their approval...
That's when I suggested our hasty removal.

Just a mile down the road, this rain of hailstones ceased
and a vacuum of silence brought a turbulent peace…
The clouds started dancing, dressed up in taffeta green
and enveloped the sky in a jungle party theme—
There they gave birth to a barbed-wire wind.
Sandy was frozen, her face had a maniacal grin,
A funnel cloud came roaring, cast down from the sky,
like the knife of the Devil, but twenty stories high!

Sandy broke from the car
in a mad, desperation run
to touch her sole fixation
this wheel where death was spun—
and I could do but nothing,
my heart came so undone
for the ghost of twenty tornadoes
swept away with twenty-one.

Friday Night

The moon must know it's Friday;
He's been drinking all night.
Crooning and swooning,
He says come dance in the half-light,
So you whirl out a step,
Choreographed by wine,
And you dance with the moon, the stars, and the stop sign.

In my mind, I see a lifetime of tonights,
But I'll keep that thought sealed tight.
And live for the moment, *that is* tonight.
There's no rain in the gutters, the moon's fully bright.
Let it shine all it's power;
I may not get another Friday night…

You whirl and a child-like wisdom glows on your face.
The moon you have embraced.
You left him spell-bound, staggered
In his starry, starry place

Round, round, round, he's spinning round you, round you,
Dancing, twirling, in a wild lunar chase,

Though the moon's all but eclipsed tonight
By curtains and candlelight,
He's tapping at me through the windowpane
In his top hat and cane.

Ashes to Dust

Wake up mother, I think he's coming home
I guess he grew tired of living on his own
And here I sit bewildered
Wondering if I've grown
Staring out the window
And waiting on the phone

You see, I believe in alibis
Broken glass and lullabies
Born was I in the Seventies
I was born to catch the sun
But I burn alive in memories
To ashes and dust I run

Wake up mother, I think he's coming home
I guess he grew tired of living on his own
And here I sit bewildered
Wondering if I've grown
Staring out the window
And waiting on the phone

And here I sit bewildered
Staring through this pane
The glass, it is still shattered
And everything remains unchanged

October Church with Confession

Fall broke like a stained-glass window—
but quietly,
and slower.

And not inside
on these hardwood floors,
resting between white walls
that reach up and up,
dividing, and dividing again
until they cradle
an impatient bell that hangs
inside a steeple…

It is Fall outside—
and in the crisp air
the trees have shattered
on the grass

and Father O'Toole is sweeping at the shards,
red maple and yellow oak,
making tiny, orchestrated piles.

"Good morning, Father."

"Good Morning, son."
His words come encased in white mist.

"Would it be too early for confession?"

"That would depend on the confession," he says,
and tidies the circumference of his last pile.

He looks up, smiling,

 "Come on in…"
and turns, his mouth trailing
white syllables.

I enter the church,

silently rehearsing the words

that I've collected

into my colorful,
manageable pile,
trimmed of the loose ends,
softened at the edges,

prepared for a tidy disposal
all its own.

Drinking You In
for Brooke, at Toad, Cambridge, Massachusetts

In this dark place,
home of the gargoyle toads,
deep red walls surround,
trapping the night's
smoke and sweat
in a cube of sound.

Harmonicas and guitars rattle our bones,
howl out their arguments
for sex, for dreams, for loneliness;
their conversation captured
in microphones,
thrown to hungry ears—
a sound track for eye contact,
body language,
touch.

Here you hold court,
pulling ales, sparking cigarettes,
dressed in a black that cannot contain your light,
(You cannot drape the moon)
so luminous,
I could read by you.

I recognize these barflies
and their courage in the face of toads.
They are moths in disguise,
fresh from cocoons,
looking for nectar,
attracted by your light,
they are hovering
around you
with me.

If You Break Down

If there comes a day
where you wish the clocks
could roll backwards;
if in the cover of night,
you're begging the stars to stay,
asking satellites
to stop and help you remember
how to picture the world
before everything had changed;

If you break down,
I'm at your shoulder.
Take me at my word,
you can break down.
I will tell you
over and over,
a reliable sound
is coming around
if you break down.
A reliable sound,
I'm coming around,
if you break down.

If fear comes
without invitation
and lays its head
in the green within your eyes;
if it's paralyzing,
I will wake you.
We will walk a thousand paces,
walk away, walk away,
till you are walking
on your own.

Millennium Poem

The 20th Century is over, but what if it never began?
What if the entire 100 years was the invention of a single man?
It was a fiction, a joke, a virtual reality hoax,
Put together by some mastermind
With some moral that's never been spoke.

In hindsight, doesn't it seem quite clear?
How could we go from a horse-drawn cart
To putting the wheel on Mars in 100 years?
He started out slowly, nineteen-ought-one-two-and-three
To pull us in quietly to the 20th Century.
But before the Wright brothers at Kitty Hawk
Had lifted off that sandy ground,
He'd invented Thomas Edison, modern medicine, electric light
And electric sound.

And then he kicked us all in the head
With the "War to End All Wars."
How could we be so gullible? Hadn't we heard that one before?
He got the Twenties roaring with drinking, dancing
And then the crash, and it would take another ten years
And the Second World War
Before our pockets found jobs and cash.

And Hitler! Good Lord, Hitler, what was he thinking there?
You put the Devil in a Chaplin moustache,
Grease back his crop-top hair and millions will follow…
How could we swallow that word for word?
That someone so evil could walk among the good people
Who inhabit this planet Earth?

And sure, he kept things spiced up a bit to keep us in the game.
He brought in Elvis, the Beatles, Aretha Franklin,

Just to drop some names.

He even gave us Bobby Dylan with a voice both sharp and flat.
(He was supposed to sound like Sinatra, but there was a misprint
Or something like that)
He framed the Sixties with sex, drugs, and rock and roll.
Assassinations, demonstrations, and shots from the grassy knoll.
He chased away Vietnam with the relative calm
Of disco and punk rock rage.
You never knew what craziness was lying
In wait from page to page.
Reaganism fought Communism
And they tore down the height of the Berlin Wall,
But he left our optimism, standing there,
Waiting for a call that never came.
Much is very different, but too much is still the same.

He shrank the computer from a warehouse to a chip.
And then he shrank the chip down till it was just a tiny blip.
And now the blip is so wee, so small it can't be seen
By the naked eye at all.

But all of us, in our little wooden house,
With our little plastic mouse,
Are glued by it to the computer screen.
Just like him, in a room that's dim,
We're all awaiting our final scene.

I know this might sound half-baked to you
This rhyming take with a hundred-year view
But I say let's override the circuits tonight
And let's write the 21st Century ourselves
And this time let's get it right...

10 Observations on Boyhood
(on the birth of Evan Jaccodine, godson)

1) All "L" shaped objects are firearms

2) Matches are for candles

3) Bleeding makes a hero

4) Dad's no barber

5) Mob Psychology starts with one

6) There are no 12-step programs for cartoons

7) It's easier to write your name in snow when you pee in cursive

8) Frog legs do not reattach

9) Never ever play the Indian

10) Yes, the girl has no penis

Lyrics

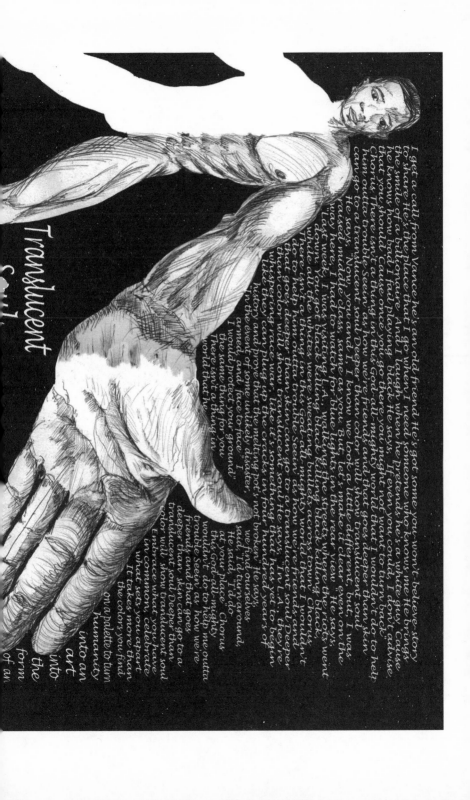

Translucent Soul

I get a call from Vance he says he's got some story to share. He's the place that I go when I need someone who knows. He brings the smile of a billionaire. And I laugh when he pretends he's a white guy, 'Cause he knows how bad I find playing black. He says, "If even you could, I don't advise that you should. 'Cause once you go there you might not want to turn back."

Chorus: There isn't a thing in this God-all-mighty world that I wouldn't do to help him outta trouble seein' a how we're friends and that goes deeper than skin. I can go to a translucent soul Deeper than color will show. Translucent.

He says, "Now, you and I know we look a little different, but, I was raised middle class, same as you. But, let's make it clear, even on the way here, I had to watch for blue lights in the rear view." He says down you got black killing black. Last week I was visiting, walking the streets where the riots went down, you got black killing black while all the white were wearing bullets across town.

Chorus: There isn't a thing in this God-all-mighty world that I wouldn't do to help him into trouble seein' a how we're friends and that goes deeper than skin. I can go to a translucent soul Deeper than color will show. Translucent.

And how we're friends and that goes deeper than skin I know we're translucent souls. In L.A. they whisper in ice war, like it's something that has yet to begin history, and prove that the cracks in our hundred years of plug up the cracks in our in the event of some unlikely disaster, armed and I face to face." I would protect your ground. There isn't a thing in the same thing for you. the melting pot's not broken. He says, we find ourselves said, "I'd turn around, at your place Chorus He said, "I'd do this God-all-mighty wouldn't do to help me outta trouble seein' as how we're friends and that goes deeper than skin can go to a translucent soul Deeper than color will show translucent soul Deeper than color will show translucent than.

Embrace what you have in common, celebrate what sets you apart. It takes more than on a palette to turn humanity the colors you find into an art into the form of an

into an
art
into
the
form
of an

Live In The Now

I've got a farmhouse,
It's a big white farmhouse,
And forty acres,
In my head.
You've got a kitchen,
It's an oak floor kitchen
And a big brass feather bed.

And there in the parlor,
An old upright piano
And a precocious blue-eyed kid
Playing the keys.

Live in the now—
A room with a view
Of Cambridge.
Live in the now—
Traffic, noise, and neighborhood kids.

We're sitting in the kitchen.
You reach across the table
And put a finger on
My wrinkled brow.

You say, "Live in the now,
Live in the now."

'Cause life is what happens
When you're busy making plans.
That's what John Lennon said,
Then he quit the fucking band.

Tell me which part—
Is it the castle, or the sand—
That you miss when the tide
Comes along?

I'm alone on a highway.
Only silos break the view.
A field of sunflowers,
A scarecrow paying dues.
And I think to myself,
"Man, that's not what I'd choose."

But here I am
And look where I've gone…
All for the song,
Till the tide
Comes along.

Live in the now—
An audience is waiting.
Live in the now—
Whose day are you creating?

I slip into the hotel.
I put the phone
On a pillow.
Your voice makes it better
Somehow.

You say, "Live in the now,
Live in the now…"

Weightless

She's trying to define her faith
   like it's some role that she's playing.
      I tell her, "You remind me of someone else..."
        But who it is, I'm not saying.

"Hear me out," she says,
   "I'm getting older,
      I don't need to justify myself to you.
        Do you hear me?"

When she walks in a room
   it's like she's walking on water
      or stepping across the moon,
        like she's gravity's only daughter.
          She's weightless, weightless.

And I say, "You're just confused
   because you talk too much to angels,
      and they faithfully refuse
        to answer questions that are painful..."

"But Faith has no weight," she says,
   "Now, Doubt, now, there's the burden...
      You're completely right to think you're grounded—
        Do you hear me?"

When she walks in a room
   it's like she's walking on water
      or stepping across the moon,
        like she's gravity's only daughter.
          She's weightless.

Last Call

You said, "Don't wait up, don't count the minutes."
So here I am watching paint fade from the walls.
On the TV, planes are dancing to the national anthem,
So the whole world knows it's long past last call.

I sat through Tarzan swinging through the jungle,
And Godzilla crushing buildings and all.
The light from this TV can make it all look so easy.
It makes this room feel incredibly small.

Last call, last call.
Now I've heard it all.
The excuses get weaker
As the stories get tall.
You step off with the wrong foot,
The drunk fool at the ball.
Well, I'm not up for dancing.
I'm up past last call.

Clock keeps on talkin'.
It says, "Fool, go to bed—
Why waste the words, they've already been said."
But I can't shut my eyes with this face in my head,
So tonight I plan on clearing my mind.

I could lay my head in the arms of the sofa,
And wait for headlights to roll across these walls.
But when your key finds the door, your feet find the floor,
They'll be greeted by empty rooms and empty halls.

Ghosts

All around me
I see ghosts,
Hanging out on balconies mostly.
Laughing at the mortals,
Like we're the brunt
Of an inside joke.
Sweet revenge that we can touch,
Our friends and family.

I see ghosts all around me.
They crash rock concerts
And the symphony.
They dress in ebony,
Like wayward funeral hosts.
Their gentle faces share their empathy.

But they don't speak to me.

It's like they see straight through me.
They know all that's to come
And what has gone.
And what frightens me
Is not their fearsome company.
It is the future that's prescribed to me.

I will not ask them why they've come.

Margaret Putnam was a nurse.
In the Civil War,
She served her country.
She walks in
Through my walls
Like an actress well-rehearsed.

She'd be more frightening
If she were less lovely...

But she won't speak to me,

It's like she sees straight through me.

She knows all that's to come
And what has gone.
And what frightens me
Is not her fearsome company.

It is the future that's prescribed to me.
I will not ask her why she's come.

I see ghosts all around me.
They sleep through lectures in theology.
They don't make apologies
For the secrets that they know.
They like to appear on *Unsolved Mysteries*.

They don't speak to me.
It's like they see straight through me.

They know all that's to come
And what has gone.
And what frightens me is not their fearsome company.

It is the future
That is prescribed to me,
So I will not ask them
Why they've come.

Trolley Car

It's a snowy night,
the cops shut down the freeway.
Big men in plows are out
carving up the streets.
Below them,
jammed on a subway,
I'm with two hundred over-dressed strangers,
brushing snow off coats
and shoulders,
kicking snow
off dress-shoe feet.

You live six miles down
this trolley car's trail,
up above the red line,
where the street musicians wail,
where, baby, we used to
chase down coffee
on the sidewalk—take in tunes.

We'd drink in
the waning hours
till we polished
off the moon.

Who knew
the moon would fail
above the trolley car trail?

"Park Street, next station,"
says a voice with an accent I've heard,
and I see shoppers on the platform
where green and red lines diverge.

I fight my way through
the packages and the bows
to a pay phone. The operator knows—
she says to me, "Your nervousness shows."
I say, "'Nervous' is too kind a word."

I think snowfall should be measured
by how much it takes
a city by
surprise,
by how far back
old-timers go
to remember
the last time a blizzard stung their eyes.
Last time I rode a subway,
you had summer in your eyes,
you did.

Your phone rings,
but it only brings
your voice
on a message machine,
"I'm not here,
the tape is clear."
Me, I'm off the hook, it seems.

"I called," I say, "to say 'hello,'
to coax you out
where the snowmen grow,
but you're not home,
and hey, I gotta go;
it was good to hear
your voice."

Changing Your Name

It was a bar room's distance
To where you ran
Your hand
Through your hair.
I was startled for an instant.
It's been six months,
A few days,
Two years.

And we laughed the laugh
Of the innocent,
As the cab cut a path
In the street. As the world
Swept by with its violence,
I thought of the first night
We fell in the sheets.

I never asked you
For nothing like changing
Your name.
I believed we had
Something here,
But nothing ever came.
Were you thrown by the language,
By words that we said?
When I told you
I loved you,
Did it get in the way?

You lit a candle,
Then you poured me
A glass of port wine.

I pulled the oven handle,
The air felt warm,
The scent
Felt kind.
And your kiss could heal
Like medicine; there ain't nothing
That it can't overcome.

But I could not lean
On this evidence,
For fear you'd take the cure
And run.
You would run...

Because love won't stop
To think about the consequences—
Turns a fool to stumbling
Over people's fences.

The moon cut a frown
Over windy town,
But you smiled
As you pulled
Down the shade,
And we turned a corner
Onto holy ground,
And got lost
In the love we made.

Bring Me Backwards

Street corner, cityside lane
People cross borders
When green lights change
And isn't that strange
A face on someone
I almost said your name
Can you blame me?
But I was foiled again

Bring me backwards
I can't fool time
I'm walking in circles
I've committed no crime
Bring on the witness
The truth is divine
You stand there bleeding
But the blood is mine

And you'd say,
"Pain is just a relative thing."
I'd say, "Thank you, Mr. Einstein."
You go on about space
This place in time
But that's no way to explain it
Believe me
When you're mining it
'Cause it's all feel
Not thought
But there I'm caught
Trying to untangle it

Deliver Me

She can turn a room 'round on a dime,
Part a crowd like the Red Sea—
She's Moses—and strangers' eyes all fall and rise
On her length like they're sizing up roses.
Delivery? She could deliver me.
She broke her own commandment—
Thou shall not steal from me.
My breath is gone, now that's burglary.
Never trust a prophet in a party dress.

I'm here waiting on a train.
There are things that I can't explain,
Like how I got tied to the tracks,
And why love goes down like some robbery—deliver me.

There's a punch line on the sidewalk,
But the joke seems kind of cruel.
It's the ones your friends aren't telling
That make you look the fool.
So you step out into traffic, 'cause it's safer on the street.
You react to perfect strangers, as if the world's complete.
It's when you're anonymous, you can pull the wool over all of us,
But when you lean, don't fall on us, broken more or less.

Have you ever been ashamed? Have you ever been defeated?
Crying, calling out her name, like love can never be repeated.
The whole world's bringing you down,
For a million different reasons.
It's just the end of one more season,
Where love came to run you down.

Independence Day

I'll shed some light on the mystery
Of why I kicked her out on Independence Day

With the fireworks burning
I found myself learning
Couldn't lay in my bed the same way
Stand by me, that's what she said
If the shithitthefan
Would you stand by me
Stand by me
Well, here I am
Here I am

6 o'clock in the city
The shade was fighting back
With the morning sun
Then the alarm started ringin'
Her curls fell 'round her
She asked me when the buses run
And the phone's been ringing since Monday
She's looking for a place where she can talk all alone
But here I am
Here I am

I know your tricks, your magic
But I don't know what your truth is about
If you paint the daylight tragic
You're never gonna figure it out
Out...

From a chair in the kitchen
I watched her live her life in a batting cage

Swingin' through jobs
Through her family
Then it hit me
It grabbed me
She's winding up like Satchel Page

And I could hear the crash
Of the fireworks
Bringing in the light
Through the windows and doors
It lit a little matchbox
Found in the kitchen
I read the name and number
And I fell on the floor

But here I am
Here I am
Here I am

I know your tricks, your magic
Now I know just what your truth is about
If you paint the daylight tragic
You're never gonna figure it out
Out…

Stand by me
That's what you said
You said you'd stand by me
Stand by me
Here I am
Here I am

Dream of New Orleans

There's me
Tripping on a cloud
I'm laughing, tumbling down
I've fallen on your doorstep
New Orleans
It stretches beneath my feet

I am the king of Bourbon Street
I strike a match
And all the street lights catch
There's you
Dancing on a roof
You say you love me 100 proof

You move inside a nightgown
Reveal yourself to the town
A trumpet speaks
Its voice rising up over Bourbon Street
You ride the sound
And throw your love on down

Mrs. Jones

Mrs. Jones wakes up, got a lover in her bed.
She don't even know the boy's last name.
And whatever excuse she makes up
For what happened in the sheets,
Lord knows, some things have got to change.

Cover me
With rose petal kisses.
Smother me
With wet perfume.
Hover over me
Like you're pulling at the ocean,
Tugging at the sand,
Oh, sweet Gravity's hands
Fill me like the light fills the moon.

Headlights in the driveway.
Somebody's in a car, a door slams,
Clip clop, your man's come home.
There's a tumble, there's a shakeup,
A knife falls to the floor.
Goddamn, that turns marrow to bone.

There's a man inside the parlor,
His heartbeat paints the floor.
A voice on his shoulder is whisperin' his name.
In the heart of a desperate hour,
Love knocks down all doors,
Knowing too well it's too late to lay blame.

She Loves A Girl

You grew up thinking you knew her
Nothing could keep you apart
You remember nothing peculiar
Your sister always spoke from the heart
You took your parents' religion
And you drank it down like a coke
It helped to quench your confusion
Now look whose heart that it broke

She loves a girl
She loves a girl
She loves a girl
What are you gonna do—
If you love her too?

A gold-and-white invitation
Your parents will not attend
They put a knife to the blood line
When the couple became more than friends
The preacher sang "Hallelujah"
But it rang more like a curse
One love at the cost of another
Man, that's when love really hurts

So take a seat
In the world of the open minded
And when you speak, tell them
Even love can be blinded
You think more of the future
When change brings your past to an end
Use your love like a suture
That's a good place to begin

Beautiful World

I was born in a taxicab.
The driver cut the cord while the meter was running.
A baby's voice crying
Up to city lights.
The papers ran the photo the next day.
Me and my mama and the cabby all smiling,
Even the Governor called to say…

Ain't it the strangest world?
It's wild and it's dangerous.
It's soft as a pearl.
Bring on the changes.
Ain't it a beautiful world?
A beautiful world, a beautiful world.

A friend of mine took
An old jetliner.
He and his girl were trying to figure out their future.
They headed off on some weekend getaway.
The plane got hit by a wall of thunder,
The fuselage bent like a wishbone nearly breaking.
He fell to knees in the aisle and proposed that day.

I want to be your medicine man, baby.
You make the call and I'll come running.
"Even in the middle of the night," you say,
"We'll fall asleep in your living room,
A candle, a blanket, and the movie we're watching,
But I would walk through fire just to touch your face."

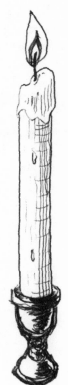

Paris in a Day

We were drunk fools in Paris, stumbling on the sidewalk
that runs along the Seine, and on the Cathedral
all the gargoyles watched us laughing,
"Two stupid Americans…"
We were at the mercy of a passionate waiter
who pulled the corks at the Osterasis Cafe.
He kept serving us wine we hadn't ordered,
then he blamed us for the weather;
it was cold and rainy—but we raised a glass up to him anyway.

We did Paris in a day, what would Marie Antoinette say?
We made a vow on the Champs Elysees
that nothing would come between us.

The Mona Lisa, I said, "She smiles just like she knows me."
you said, "She's a woman with nothing to lose—
she gathers a crowd around her, then she flirts with
perfect strangers, but she'll never take a lover in the Louvre—
she will never take a lover in the Louvre…"

We did Paris in a day, what would Quasimodo say?
Would he stand on top of Notre Dame and throw down tourists to us?

A thousand stairs up the Pompadou,
we were gasping at the view.
If we tried for Jim Morrison's gravesite too,
we'd probably have to find a tour bus, and man,
how do we find a tour bus without finding another day?

We took the M across the Seine and headed for the Eiffel Tower
and there the street merchants called us out by name,
"Cool shades here for the Americans,"
they said in their finest hipster English,
and then they told us, "Every Yankee looks the same."
I said, "Is it the camera case, or our American grace?"
They said, "You all just look the same…"

We lit a candle for a ghost in the Notre Dame Cathedral.
We got lost on the Left Bank looking
for a place in which to stay.
When we told the waiter there what we had done, he said,
"Only an American would attempt Paris in a day…
Only an American would do Paris in a day…"

We did Paris in a day what would Marcel Marceau say?
We put up our feet at the Fountain Cafe
and toasted the bond between us.

We drank sherry with an Englishman.
We caught up like long-lost friends.
Under the Arc we watched the sunset end,
and laughed at the miles that had passed beneath us,
the miles that passed beneath us.
You said, "That's kilometres, baby,"
but I wouldn't let it come between us.
Nothing will come between us…

Here She Is

If you could paint her, she'd be a Picasso.
She's got a few things out of place.
Like when she smiles, it's slightly out of line.
It's half awkward, yet half grace.
While you're unraveling this mystery
Of where she fits in time and space,
She'll drag you into this lover's tale,
Though she will not give a reason.
And if you fight her tooth and nail,
She won't give up until you lose...

She wants the last word, the last dance.
She thinks it's absurd that you believe in second chances.
You're a lost cause, yet here she is.
And that's the mystery. Here she is...

She's a poem by Ferlinghetti.
She's the angel from a nursery rhyme.
She'll set you a place at your table,
Then fill your cup till you're drunk on red wine.
She don't believe in stars or in miracles,
But she reads your horoscope daily.
And if your response is too cynical,
She'll say, "Who are you to know?"

While you're unraveling this mystery
Of where she fits in time and space,
She'll memorize your history
And decorate your place.

Blizzard

Weather advisory, one for the diaries
Windy and cold so stay off the road
It's bitter outside your windows
Stack your blankets, light your candles
There isn't a phone booth, and ain't it the cold truth
It's a lonely old highway, just me and the plows
Making the most of their payday
Laying salt in the wounds of the roadways

For your bed I'll beat the cold,
With a blizzard in my headlights, or an avalanche in the road
Snow blinds every road sign,
So I'm counting the miles as I'm going
There's a shroud of black ice forming
The radio sends out ample warning...

Up on the next hill, a trailer truck load spilled
It spun in a jackknife, and now it's a still life
Framed by the flares and the cruisers,
Orange coats and one sore loser...

In hindsight, it's been a long night
And where I was, was not so cold
Another sound bite off the dash lights
It's more than a foot or so they're told

Two hundred miles to Chicago, my eyes froze to the road
Mesmerized as the windshield collides with the snow...

Weather advisory, one for the diaries
Windy and cold so stay off the road

Don't Breathe

Picture my face
At your kitchen table,
We're both fifteen years old.
Your parents are sleeping
Upstairs in their bedroom,
The house is quiet, but cold.

Did I tell you then?
These are moments
Whole lifetimes are built on.
You're my best friend,
And if it's tonight
Will these walls hold our secret?

Don't breathe out loud—
It's like breaking glass,
And the walls must hold
The moments fast...

Picture my face
In the space of your garage.
We're still fifteen years old.
Naked in blankets,
The angels would thank us,
If they knew how the future was told.

Did I tell you then?
These are moments
Whole lifetimes are built on.
You're my best friend—
And now we're skin to skin
Only sweat runs between us.

Don't breathe out loud…
Don't breathe out loud…
Don't breathe…

Hold these pieces,
Pictures in tatters.
Fade the colors,
Still a fortune to hold.
Picture my face,
In frame in a picture
Of when we were fifteen years old.
Fumbling for answers,
Two out-of-step dancers,
Content in darkness to hold.
Did I tell you then?

These are moments my whole life is built on.

You're my best friend.
Did I tell you then?
Did I tell you then?
Did I tell you?

When We Begin

The black strapless dress fits just right.
The calendar's marked six Friday night.
She puts on a little makeup,
Just enough to shake things up,
'Cause if she's moving on,
She's gonna do it right.

So tell me the story
Of all your past glories—
The lovers, the losers, the friends.
Spill all your magic,
The good times, and the tragic—
Tonight will this mystery end?
When we begin,
When we begin.

His cab driver says, "Here we are."
It's pouring outside on the boulevard.
But he smiles as he tips him,
Though a nervousness grips him,
He looks up at the place
And pulls the door ajar.

She takes one last glance in the mirror.
He shakes himself off on the stairs.
He's fixing up the flowers,
She's looking up at the hour.
They both make a wish
for one good-night kiss.
He's knocking at the door…

Give In, Give Up

If I fell down on my knees
If I came to you pleading
Would you take me as I am
Your touch is all I'm needing

Bring me courage, bring me change
We'll find oxygen in rain
And build a shelter in these arms
If this love should come to harm

You know who I am
Put a little faith in me
If you need some space on a shoulder

Why? Why? Why do we fall so fast—
Take your ghosts into battle
Is your heart made of glass?
Just give in, give up
Get ready for this
Give in, give up, get ready for it…

'Cause I am whispering your name
It colors in the rain
Bells are ringing in this town
The women walk in wedding gowns
And if you fear your bones may break
If it comes to heart aching
The dance comes down to this
Every love will bring a risk

The colors you choose
Are yellows and blues
Let's paint the sky, over and over

Words

Words are better when they're written down
They fall to the page with no sound.
And if you let them sit awhile,
Give them time and distance.
You won't hear the rattle in the voice
That gives a fool away with no choice.
Time is all you have tonight,
So take the time and get this right.

Your eyes make me humble,
I fall down at your feet.
Pick me up if I stumble
Over words I cannot speak.
I can't speak…

And so I'm mining an empty page
For the words I've got to say.
The sun brings another day and here I am still reaching.
I hear the sigh of a morning train.
I watch it waking you up again.
These words I can't explain,
But here I am still speaking…

You say, if you doubted me,
That you'd take all that was yours and you'd go,
So take what you've given me,
If these words don't voice what a heart just knows…

I just can't speak…
I just can't speak…
I just can't speak…
Speak…

Rollaway Bed

Wake up Gracie
You're stealing the covers again
It's 4 in the morning
December's outside creeping in
Now 1000 times over I love you
1001 now it's said
But if I want to sleep I've got to find you
Your very own rollaway bed

Now I'm a night person
Come home late from playing the bars
You're tossing and turning
Spinning like Saturn and Mars
At 8 in the morning you wake me
With your coffee, your jam, and your bread
You'd be less likely to burn me
In your very own rollaway bed

Saturday we wake up
We're driving round town
Trying to find the perfect bed
You fall on the mattress
You faint like an actress
The salesmen are all turning red

Move over Gracie
I can't face sleeping alone
Without all that tossin'
It don't even feel like I'm home
Now 1000 times over I love you
1002 now it's said
Baby I don't mean to wake you
But is there room in the rollaway bed?

Drop of Your Name

When I'm older, the cane holder
When crossing the street ain't the same
I'll avoid street sweepers, the grim reaper
Calling me out by my name

When I'm weary, when I'm older
When the world has grown colder
I'll wear my pride like a soldier
At the drop of your name

And you, you'll be making me lists again
I'm the grocery clerks best friend
He says, "Say hello to the Missus."
And though my mind be there just in pieces
It still never ceases
To be amazed by my luck with you…

And the sidewalk, if it could talk
If it could trace me back with colored chalk
It would take me round and round the block
To every place I've been with you
To small cafes where we lost whole days

To nights in bars in a whisky haze
To a Saturday church parade where everyone
Just stared at you

And the weary old soldier
In a world that's grown colder finds the will to move forward
At the drop of your name, the drop of your name
The drop of your name

The Art of Distance

You get the call on the message machine.
It's 2 am—it better be important.
Her power's out, it's a sleep-walk 'cross town.
Rain's coming down, she's got candlelight and blankets.
Is this an act between friends?
One step forward, two steps back again.

If you knew the art of distance,
Would you lay in your bed
Or take a cab across town?
You know it's raining right now.
You crave her skin, well,
You crave its resistance.
When you wake up in the morning
And she's asking for time,
You give in.
She's the queen of light and candles.
You give in, you always were a sucker
For a scandal.

You ring her bell,
She buzzes you in.
Brush off the rain,
You give her the umbrella
When she comes to you,
Wrapped in her sheets.
Is she beautiful?
How you gonna tell her?
When the touch begins,
You cradle her face.
Is this the betrayal of a friend?

Maria's Beautiful Mess

She fell to the mattress
With the grace of an actress.

You're falling like a thief from a roof.

She's asking for proof—
"Are you staying?"
Outside you hear mission bells.

Welcome to Maria's beautiful mess,
In a cluttered apartment on the West Side.
She pulls the blinds,
While you watch how
Her dress falls
Around her.

And the world slows,
A clock shows a wrinkle
In the flow of time.
And she steps close,
Her eyes glow, lips pop open
Like a bottle of wine.

And she loves
Like it's thirst,
Like she's never
Been hurt.
She dances just like
Nobody's watching.
Is this love? Is this cursed?
It feels like the first time, falling,
Nobody's watching, nobody's watching.

Now, she puts on some music.
She asks you to choose it.
You sang her back a Gershwin line.

Now Ella is singing,
Holy,
Soulfully,
Bringing up better times.

And beneath the tunes,
She's smiling
On an unmade bed.
She says—
"What's in the middle
That scares you?
Does it dare you
To take a moment
And just slow down?"

Pull the curtains all down,
Let the stars fall around you,
She's smiling
Like the Mona Lisa.

You could conquer this town
If your feet touched the ground,
But you're falling, boy,
I know, I see you,

I see you,
I see you.

This Old Car

This old car has seen the ages since the second of the world wars
Bought by a Jersey family on the cutting edge of poor
A ragged wife and weary children, stricken with the chore
Of a restless man of thirty-five, who dreamed he lived for more...

I'm hating my surroundings and my soul I'm sure is dead
I will die a hollow, bitter man with a gun against my head
I need some time to drive alone, to feel the wind
and the life I've blown
I may be back, but don't expect it
This car will find me home

After two-thousand turns of the gauge, he hid his wedding band
And lost the keys in a musty room to lust and a woman's hand
She stole-off with her lover—
He was a dressed-up blues harp man
And they chased the roads to Chicago for the blues
From any raging band

This old car has seen the ages,
since the second of the world wars
It's seen a man in his final stages, seen two lovers opening doors
But the doors jammed shut and struck up the band
When the blues man asked for more
The woman heard no harmony in the blues
Of old Chicago lore

In a back field in a farmer's lot, a boy-man finds the car
Bought for a song by his father, it's been ten years off the tar
A motionless engine is a curse
To a boy with a ready heart
In a boxed-up town where dreams abound
But never get their start

Autobiography of a Pistol

I'm a pistol, a forty-five;
I just shot two men in this hot-house dive.
Now I'm smoking-burning hot barrel of metal.
Believe it or not, I was bought by this guy named Ray,
a card-carrying member of the NRA,
But he left me out in his car one day,
And now the finger on my trigger hasn't seen
its sixteenth birthday.

Some things they never tell you
when you're riding the assembly line.
Like who'll be the hands to hold you
and what's their state of mind—
Hey, I'm not much bigger than a pointed index finger.
So who am I to lay the blame?
I'm only here to cause some pain…

The sirens—
I can hear them, they're singing…
They're singing my song,
"When the sun sets, I get upset—
Darkness fills me and I want to light up the world…"

Would you believe I've seen better days?
I starred in westerns and won rave reviews.
Now I sit on a shelf, tagged for judgment day.
I've got to change the jury's point of view.
You see, guns don't kill people, it's the bullets that do.
I said guns don't kill people,
Bullets do.
Yeah, the bullets do…

All My Heroes Were Junkies

In 1968, he did shots with the Doors at the Whiskey-A-Go-Go.
It was on one of those hot Hollywood summer nights.
He says, "Jimmy came in tight leather slacks, it was hot as hell
But we were drinking Jack, his eyes were like quarters,
Round, and black when he stepped under the stage lights…"
"And you know me," he says, "I had pawned my only camera.
I had no way to record these fleeting Kodak moments
That sprung to life each and every Saturday night.
I was too far gone back then to have known it…"

He says, "All my heroes were junkies,
Now all my heroes are dead."
I say, "Hey Tony, consider yourself lucky
To be a junkie in a hospital bed."

He says, "You know, Judy Garland never showed up
When I took my walk in the Land of Oz,
Though a cop did on a purple horse one morning.
He asked me why I was staggering,
I said—because—because, because, because
The wizard never gave me no Surgeon General's Warning."

"Who rolled the joint when Bob Dylan
Got high with the Beatles?" He says,
"Who put my world on pins and needles?"
He tells the nurses they should do something
With the ceiling in the rehab ward,
Like paint a fresco to the late-great Betty Ford.
They come in and make their jokes about
Pulling out all his power chords.
He tells them, "Could you come up with
Something I didn't already know?"

Martyr's Lounge

Leo's is the bar up in heaven
Where all the martyrs hang out
Gandhi staggers in with John Lennon
They'll start a bar fight, no doubt

When you lead, we follow
When you bleed
Oh, the masses feel your pain
Plant your seed, setting sunflowers
Growing inside our brains...

Now, Jesus don't need
No introduction
He's got a famous Old Man
And a party of twelve
I see Cobain
He's well;
He's in the Angels That Fell
A local touring bar-band.

JFK
Joan of Arc
Sit in the corner
Kissing in the dark
Marilyn Monroe
Jacques Cousteau
Talk about the sharks
They used to know...

Medicine

Marilyn Monroe bought a bungalow
In sunny West Hollywood.
She took to the bottle; she threw out Aristotle,
'Cause the thinking wasn't doing no good.

It's a goddamn waste; it's a bitter taste,
The pills we pop, the drinks we chase.
She threw down the script; she threw down the bottle.
Now who's gonna call Joe Dimaggio?

You're dressed for the fight;
It's a Saturday night on the boulevard,
And I can hear in your voice,
You're making bad choices.
Man, you only call me when it gets hard.
And we ask you to change,
And ain't it strange how friends disappear?
We're tired of steering you clear,
Go ahead, fall all apart.

In boys town, they party 'round the clock.
The clock is spinning backwards.
The jesters doubletalk.
And if you listen to your language,
You could break the fall
Of rhymes and steal back time…

If we took the medicine away,
Would the walls you build hold against the day?
When the sky is falling, when heaven's calling,
When you run from your past, your future is stalling.
You find your grip and hold against the day…
Heaven holds a place for those who pray.

River

While Hollywood sleeps,
A young man is dying
On the concrete of a sidewalk downtown.
As his brother weeps,
The sirens come calling
And the medics feed him lines on the ground.
Run, river, run...

The director speaks;
The cameras are rolling.
A boy steps between
The backdrop and the lights.
And he's stealing the scene,
With the crew as his witness.
The whole industry will judge him
Come academy night.

Now the tabloids will say what they want to,
And the cameras will re-enact his fall.
His legacy speaks, but no one can hear it,
'Cause his death has made critics of us all.
His legacy speaks

In the canister rooms,
In the archives of great studio halls.
And there it will keep,
Like a secret that's whispered
Between lovers
And those who never knew him at all.

Angel

Needle in my hand
Got a forearm rubber band
Got a golden liquid in a tube
I'm gonna do a vessel jam
Got lots of money
Got lots and lots and lots of time

I think, I think I might be
I think, I think I am
I think, I think I might be
I think, I think I am

It's like liquid sunshine
Fire and rain
Marmalade skies
Far away eyes glazed
In a haze of cocaine

Angel's on the corner,
He's got ten vials in his hands
He sells each one for ten dollars
Like some medicine man
Seems to know alot
For a kid just sixteen years old
He's a four-year veteran
Of the penal code

He's got trademark shoes
Three tattoos
A brass-chord necklace
And a smoke-stack, too

There's a black wind
Spinning the city's weathervanes
And the eye of the storm
Is a crystal of cocaine
Can't you hear the wind?
Can't you see the driving rain
Take a break from the storm
In the eye of the hurricane?

Eyes
In the mirror
Not too sure if they're my own
Black-white eyes
In the mirror
On a face of cold stone
Black-white eyes
Riddles and lies
They tell me, tell me, tell me

You've got nothing

To hide

But...

The Ball is Coming Down

In the city by the river
a man is standing on a bridge
His eyes to Heaven to the Forgiver
who flips the coins on who should live
A naked light bulb in the corner
naked Mary's in an unmade bed
spilling champagne on her lover
forgot his name
"What had he said?"

It's New Year's Eve
Tonight in the city
they're tearing the chandeliers down
Boys and girls
all dressed up pretty
the bartenders buying the round
You count your blessings
you say your prayers
Kiss an acquaintance
the ball is coming down

Sadie Hawkins
she left the ballroom
mascara running from a fight
She slaps the doorman's face
in the lobby
He'd only asked her
"Are you all right?"
Charlie Jenkins
makes resolutions like
"Do not drink," and "Do not fight"
His conscience needs absolution
it keeps him up when it's late at night

Say Something

Carrie's a cold one, colder than the winter sun;
I should warn you, you better dress for it.
And I'm not the only one that thinks so.
Beauty is skin deep, and yes, she is thick-skinned,
But what's that for virtue?

You want her to say some,
Say something, say anything,
Or say nothing at all…
Say some, say something, say anything,
Or say nothing at all…

She's browsing for postcards,
Staring back at the cover girls on the magazines.
Even the clerk is checking her out.
She's unaware that she owns the scene,
Though everyone goes out of their way for her.

And all her life reads like some fairy tale,
But her world is so frail.
What did I tell you,
She never looks out her window
To see the setting sun.
You tell her the skies are blue;
She'll say the storms will come
Because every day is rain, every day is rain…

You want her to say some,
Say something, say anything,
Or say nothing at all…
Say some, say something, say anything,
Or say nothing at all…

Paperback Man

So she's lost inside this novel
Somewhere between 200 pages
She knows the characters by their faces
She lives the dialogue line by line

And if she could she'd never finish
She don't even know the title
Pulp Fiction or the Bible
Either argument could stand

I don't breathe anymore
She gives the world her final notice
This is what words are down here for
Let's give them the benefit of purpose

She enters the world of the paperback man
The streets are all fiction, just believe what you can
I pick up her suitcase, declare who I am
Pleased to meet you, I am the paperback man
I am the paperback man

I will never let you down

And now she sleeps beneath my blankets
Her skin is warm, her flesh inviting
It feels like I'm the one who is writing
It feels like I am the one who is real

But a crooked man is waiting
He's in the ink that marks these pages
He's in the writer's blood and he rages
He is a killer with eloquent lines

If I could breathe, I'd do more
I'd beg the editors for justice
Is this what words are down here for?
To kill her off from some high-rise office?

She's entered a world
Of the paperback man
The streets are all fiction,
Humanity's banned
I'd kill to protect her
'Cause that's who I am
Pleased to meet you,
I am the paperback man
I am the paperback man

King of 7th Avenue

I can count all the lights in the city
from the ledge on the twenty-seventh floor.
There must be ten thousand windows or more.
It's a hobby I can count on,
Helps me forget about the cold.
And I get to meet the neighbors
For as long as the ledge will hold.

In the window across from me,
A man is committing a robbery.
It's another form of the New York City Lottery.
His ears must be burning,
He drops the bag and he stares.
I'm the man out on the building.
Yes, there's no net down there…

And there's a woman below that I see.
Her silhouette is quite beautiful.
It plays tricks on my memory.
Puts a face on the shadows in front of me.
A crowd below is forming, beneath this
window ledge, my throne.
I am the King of Seventh Avenue,
New York City is my home.

I think the sirens have come for me,
Their searchlights reach up to the balcony.
They bathe me in light, blind me so I can't see.
I hear the crowd all ask for jumping,
While the cops all ask for calm.
Even the pigeons think I'm something,
The whole city is in my palms.

And there's a woman below that I see.
Her silhouette is quite beautiful.
It plays tricks on my memory.
Puts a face on the shadows in front of me.
A crowd below is forming, beneath this
window ledge, my throne.
I am the King of Seventh Avenue,
New York City is my home.

My daughter Lisa says to me,
"Dad the world is yours, and it's beautiful.
Don't throw it all away on memories.
You've got to meet new people…"
Yeah, that will be good for me.
Good for me.
Good for me.

So I watch the lovers behind their shades.
I've seen them embrace after their furious fights.
I've watched them mend their fences,
Make their love all night.
Only to tear them down again,
Change the limits,
Change the boundaries.
The same beginning, the same end.
Yet the story still astounds me.
The whole world now is watching.
From this window ledge, my throne,
I'm the King of Seventh Avenue.
And tonight I'm not alone.
I'm not alone.

3,000 Miles

My name is Robert Wilson,
I'm from Eau Claire, Wisconsin.
I've been living out of a suitcase now for fourteen days…
I walked the boulevard in Hollywood,
I caught a Vegas show that was no good—
Met a dancer there that starred in a Broadway play.
But it's a lonely world from this Greyhound,
Believe me, I've been here fourteen days.

Three thousand miles,
I've been here fourteen days,
Three thousand miles…

Now twenty-one is as good a guess as any age that I'd confess to,
Let's just say I'm old enough to get away.
Back in school, I found the only written truth
On bathroom stalls and telephone booths.
I studied awhile, but college got in my way.
I've learned much more from the back of this Greyhound,
Believe me, I've been here fourteen days.

Three thousand miles,
I've come a long, long way,
Three thousand miles…

Have you seen?
The world outside is turning—
And it's yours—
We were put here for the learning.
People talk to themselves on Greyhounds,
Even the driver strains to hear
They tell the same forgotten story—

Will it fall on forgetful ears?

Down in Houston on comes this woman
With two kids and a bottle of booze,
And she cracked them both like match heads
Whenever they ventured too close to her fuse.

And I sat with a girl from Boston,
Playing cards for cigarettes.
I lost her name with the poker game,
But her face I will never forget—
You never forget the view from these windows,
Believe me, I've been here fourteen days...

Three thousand miles,
I've come a long, long way,
Three thousand miles...

My name is Robert Wilson.
I'm from Eau Claire, Wisconsin. I've been living out
of my suitcase now for fourteen days. I walked
the boulevard in Hollywood. I caught a Vegas show
that was no good—met a dancer there who starred
in some Broadway play.

My name is Robert Wilson.

Look at the Wind Blow

I'm only seventeen, but I want much more
Than a small town girl should bargain for
More than standing in one place
Waiting for the next James Dean
I live in a town that's gripped in the Bible Belt
Man, I bared my back and I took the welts
I only pray to get out of here
Maybe someday I'll find out if the world is green

There is nothing to do in this town at night
But sit in my car and watch the streetlights
Or stare out the window at the pizza joint
What's the point?
I wish I could buy my Ford a sail
Hey, hey, look at the wind blow

Now the life of the local beauty queen
Is tied to the captain of the baseball team
They got a baby on the way
At least that's what the kids are saying
And the wedding I'm told, well it must take place
To save both families from disgrace
But the whole town knows
You see, it ain't like she's not showing…

Tommy Bates sits in his car and he waits
For his girl down at Lucky's Diner
They're at the end of the loop and he's drinking soup
While she puts on more eyeliner
I passed them once, and I'll pass them twice
And I'll pass them back again
They bought an old Range Rover from the next town over
And their headlights are my friends…

Seize the Day

She comes to my bed like a whisper
Slips in the sheet like a ghost
Says to my ear, "Hey mister,
You need to take this girl to the coast."
I need to kick up my feet in the ocean
Feel the taste of salt sea spray
Baby, let's live in the moment
'Cause it feels like life is taking the moment away

Let's Seize the day, Seize the day, Seize the day

In the kitchen in the morning
She pours coffee in my favorite cup
She's been dancing on the linoleum—barefoot
The squeaking nearly woke me up
She put Tom Jones on the stereo
Now that I could do without
Ah, but who needs perfection?
I like the tension when there's room for doubt…

Seize the day, Seize the day, Seize the day
Seize the day, Seize the day, Seize the day

She brought some pens, a couple of notebooks
A postcard, a blanket, a bottle of Merlot
And the sky provided the sunset
Me—I brought the music of Nat King Cole
"And I'd come back as a sea-gull," I said,
"If in the next life they'd give you the choice…"
"I'd come back with ya—we could go flying,"
She said, "You'd hear me raise my voice, too…"

Seize the day, Seize the day, Seize the day

Sweet Mistakes

Pop the cork,
A champagne glass,
Raise to the future,
Drink to the past.
Thank the Lord for the friends he cast,
In the play he wrote for you.

And if you love the girl,
Man, light up a torch,
Blaze a trail to her front porch.
Kiss her till your lips are scorched,
Till the rain comes down on you.

Bless your sweet mistakes,
That crumbled you down to your knees,
That brought you to this place,
Changing you by degrees…

When change was just what you needed…

So if you live your life
In a three piece suit,
In a cocktail dress,
Or combat boots,
You pick your path,
You walk your truth,
And the world will come 'round to you.

It's a long ride; I can't tell you why,
But there's a place in your pocket
Where peace can abide.
You pull it out,
It's a compass, a guide,

And it will put a little soul on you.

And in this wild blue world,
There is a soul weavin' fine-feelin' girl.
You've got to walk in paradise
To find a pearl.
If you only believe,
You'll get what you need…

What you needed…

Conquer your fear
And you'll master the game;
Life is always and never the same.
Use a little faith
To light the flame
And I know you'll connect to you.

Pop the cork,
A champagne glass,
Raise to the future,
Drink to the past.
Thank the Lord
For the friends he cast,
In the play he wrote for you.

Take Me Down

I'm a one-man line
at the twenty four-hour store
I'm in a town that reminds me
of my home town streets
I roamed the aisles a thousand miles
from what I was looking for
A familiar face that would
smile at me sweetly

If you
Take me down
To where I'm whole
Where everybody knows me
Deep as a soul can go
If you take me down
I gotta know
Did you really know me,
Deeply
As a soul can go?

We'd drive up the canyon
To watch the stars fall down
Watch them turn off the lights on the church
Down on second street
There's Jack's old man,
He's still the only cop in town
He's patrolling the sidewalk
On the graveyard beat

And everybody needs a place to call home
A roof overhead a bed for dreams of their own
I've never been so lonely as when I told you I was leaving
This time I'm really leaving

Seventeen Septembers

Do you remember
17 Septembers ago
Sweat on the backseat
Dylan on the radio
You peeled off your troubles
When you peeled off your old blue jeans

But in the dash light
She's like an angel fallen to earth
And you convince yourself that she's worth
Every risk you took the night the cornfields shook
Bye, bye baby, in the click of hands
Hello yet-to-be mystery man
One night in a car changed who you are

A boy at the front wheel
17 Septembers have passed
"Pop the clutch with your left heel…"
You're linking up his future, your past
And you tell him, "Your mom and me were bound for trouble—
Wedding bells at the age of 18…"

But in the dash light
He looks like an angel fallen to earth
And now you know how it could have been worse
For every risk you took the night the cornfield shook

Bye, bye baby, in the click of a hand
Look he's a yet-to-be mystery man
Who played kick-the-can
With a glass filled with sand

Did I Ever Know You?

So, you found yourself a corner apartment
With a view of the town all your own
All your friends say
The city's gonna kill you
Or cure you

Five flights of stairs to your home
And even now
It's changed how you walk
In the street
Past cabbies
And chimney sweeps
Be careful
With strangers
You speak to

What has this city done to you?
Has it taken the small town out of you
And turned you into someone I never knew?

When we were kids
In the warmth of a porch light
You'd smuggle out twin cigarettes

We'd blow smoke in the air
With typical hometown flair
Two futures we could not predict

And look at you now
The dreamer with the back porch plan
For the writer and the music man
Our faces on magazine stands

What has this city done to you?
Has it taken the innocence out of you
And turned you into someone I never knew?
Did I ever know you?

Do you know how
You light up these buildings?
You can turn the head
Of a man whose grown old
You're a candle
When the streets grow cold

I can hear a cricket
In your fifth-floor apartment
It's 3 am
Back home he'd put me to sleep
But he's fighting to be heard
He can't get in a word
'Cause there's a fool
Laughing outside in the street

Where are you now?
I lost you out on Montague Street
To the city that never will sleep
Is it the sideshow in you
That it speaks to?

Hey did I ever know you?
Did I ever know you?

All Things Being the Same

She is searching for some form of salvation
In the corner of a bar down the street,
But the gin controls whole conversations
And plays magic tricks with her feet…
She gets up, falls down, breaks even,
Gets caught by the wrong mister right—

Hey, it's a hard town.
I wouldn't want to live in it—
But I wouldn't want to give up in it,
All things being the same…

Back home she's got these pictures on her mirror,
They frame her when she looks back at her face.
They tell her where she's been—
I'll tell you where she's going,
She's got her name on a stool down at Eddie Owen's place…

She drinks when romance brings her down.
Like the sight of blood is a wedding gown.
Bright lights and smoke fill up this space.
It's a crowded room, but still a lonely old place…

All her friends are nothing more than strangers,
Whose names are just words on a face.
If they bumped into her out on a sidewalk on some Sunday,
They wouldn't recognize her outside of the place.

Never Lived at All

Becky's playing a piece by Gershwin on her old piano
She's been playing since her childhood, too long to recall,
But the chords that fall from her fingertips are the same
she played when she could barely sit still, back in '69,
when the keys made her hands look small
And she built her dream around symphonies and concertos
around traveling the country, and playing the music halls
Four kids later the dream's been reduced to "what-if" scenarios
but hey, to never dream is to have never lived at all
Never lived at all

Dave's a corporate lawyer in the city of Chicago
and for fifteen years, he's had his nose to the old grindstone
poured his money in the bank to feed the beast called portfolio
Well, if time is money, then success is a life alone
He looks out at the skyline for some forgiveness
When you invest in love, the same will be returned
He prided himself on a lifetime of spoken directness
It took him forty years to hear the lesson learned
Has he never lived at all?
Never lived at all...
Never lived at all

The great American novel sits on top of Peter's kitchen table
300 pages on a town he built inside of his head
He signs the cover page, uncorks the bottle with the dusty label,
pours his wife a glass, she says "Baby, bring the bottle to bed."
At 6 am he's out fighting the cars on the freeway
and fighting his manuscript; has he written his own downfall?
But he'll embrace rejection; he'll kiss the seal of each envelope
Better to live in hope than to never have lived at all
To never live at all
Never live at all

Did Galileo Pray?

When he looked into a starry sky upon Jupiter,
With its cold moons making their weary rounds,
Did he know that the Pope
Would claim that he ran with Lucifer
And a prison cell would be where he'd lay his head down?

Was he wearing a thorny crown?
When he plotted the motion of planets,
Was Mercury in retrograde?
But he found the truth when a lie was what was demanded.
When the judges asked him pointedly,
He was trembling that day.

Did Galileo pray?

And he said, "Tell Ptolemy, tell Copernicus,
That the Sun is at the core of us."
The Church, the Pope can't deny the Milky Way.

And every flower that follows the sun
Has known all along what God had done.
They whisper truth as the seasons each give way.
In the heavens you'll see it as God has conceived it.
Believe, believe it. What have you got to do to believe?

Don't shoot the messenger,
When the postman brings you truth today.
'Cause truth will march in Birmingham.
It'll block the tanks in Tiananmen,
Put the judges on the witness stand.
Let's see what they all say.

Last at the Table

Preacher, won't you preach to me?
I need a pint of philosophy.
I'm hurt and thirsty, set me on my way.
Mondays come and Mondays go,
But this one seems to be sort of slow.
Can you tell me sir, when will there come a change?

I'm the one who's last at the table;
I'm the one who never gets the gold.
You're the one who says I'm able,
But you turn your words with lies and fables…

Mothers, won't you cry for me?
I'll sell your tears for a token fee
On a street corner where drunk patrons stand laughing.
And they'll stop; they'll stare at me,
Scratch at their heads, "How can this be?"
I'll say, "I was born like you—"
then I'll startin dancin'…

Hello, Mr. Bureaucrat.
You pick who's thin—you pick who's fat.
Now, what makes you so fit for the shoes you walk in?
In an office space, you get a taste
For paper money and paper waste.
Now, who gets what depends on who is talking…

Everything's Broken

She went alone to the movies to escape into Hollywood's hands.
The screen color's soothing,
Can lift a mood like the weatherman,
And her lover is asleep on his cross.
He's playing the martyr for the dreams that he's lost.

She just can't keep out the rain or the rust,
'Cause everything's broken, everything's broken.

Well, you've just got to breathe,
Throw the weight off the table,
Watch china break up in mid-air…
But I can't help you leave—
You gotta walk on a cable.
Each step's gonna bring you somewhere…

She wakes up and the theater's bare.
A coffee shop at midnight,
She befriended a novelist there.
The plot thickens with daylight.
She hides a bruise beneath a lock of her hair.
And ain't it a paradox, you find love and get lost.
I walked her home on Winter Street,
Knowing boundaries were crossed.
You pay the rent but you don't know the cost
Till everything's broken…
Till your last friend has spoken.

Well, you've just got to breathe,
Throw the weight off the table,
Watch china break up in mid-air.
She watched herself leave,
Took a walk on a cable,

Each step's gonna bring her somewhere.
She walks up her Winter Street stair.
Hey, hey, hey, hey, yeah…

Now she's dressed like a riddle;
She's pretty as a turn of a phrase.
She's pierced in the middle;
She'll catch your eye like a misplaced parade.
And in my living room, she's falling apart.
The tale is a tragedy; it's Shakespeare's lost art.
You find your voice
When you're most torn apart,
When everything's broken…
When your own lips have spoken.

Well, you've just got to breathe,
Throw the weight off the table,
Watch china break up in midair…
She watched herself leave,
Took a walk on a cable—
Each step's gonna bring her somewhere,
A thousand feet in the air.
And ain't that a breeze up there?
Up there…
Up there…

Angel In Manhattan

Tell the man who repairs the wings for angels
That one has fallen among the mortals on Bleecker Street
I lent a hand; she looked up at the steeples
As if to blame them for the pavement beneath her feet
She said, "I never much liked flying, but the job requires trying
The hard part's avoiding buildings and concrete."

Spread the news, 'cause there's an angel in Manhattan
Call out the paparazzi and the television crews
Let the people choose
Would a little Faith come to harm them?
Print the headlines up in the *New York Daily News*
It was just another day
Like any other, other day
A Tuesday afternoon

I hailed a cab, a crowd gathered as it pulled beside us
And somebody tore at her wings, but I helped her safely inside
"I'm much obliged," she said, but the driver he looked shaken
He said, "You're fakin', lady, who's taking who for a ride?"
But then we floated up over the traffic
She turned the radio to static
And she sang to him in Billie Holiday's sweet voice

Spread the news, 'cause there's an angel in Manhattan
Call out the paparazzi and the television crews
Hey, if you choose
Would a little Faith come to harm you?

Print the headlines up in the *New York Daily News*
It was just another day
What will the mayor say?
"Good afternoon."

We flew down the length of Fifth Avenue
She threw out miracles; it was a hysterical ride
And if the crowd on the sidewalk looked skeptical
She took the blue right out of their cynical eyes
"It's all in what you feel inside."

She shook the mayor's hand, and he declared
That he'd hold a press conference
The fans and protesters blocked the stairs to city hall
"I'd like to thank you all," he said
And when she stepped before the cameras
It felt like a trial, but she smiled as the questions were called
"What do you say to detractors,
Who claim you're just some actor?"
She said, "The question here is, 'Do I believe in you?'"
It was just another day, like any other, other day

Spread the news, I saw an angel fly from Manhattan
In front of paparazzi, in front of television crews
And me I choose; I know a little Faith wouldn't harm me
Despite what they print in the *New York Daily News*
It was just another day, like any other, other day
Like any day

Lay Your Wager Down

You're my flesh and blood
But we're not the same
a common name
and now
a common distance
I looked up to you
in your plush armchair
respect or fear
I couldn't see the difference

Lay your wager down
Who'll be king in Tinsel Town?
'Cause all the prophets
and the gypsies
on the strip in
Venice Beach
have looked me in the eye
and said
"Your dreams still lie in reach."

And who am I to doubt them
and who are you
to write these speeches?

Is it my poverty
that brings a blush to you?
Or the honesty
that speaks the mind
that comes with it?

Were you once a man
with younger eyes
a hungry pride
that would not feel
resistance?

Lay your wager down
They're crowning the king
in Tinsel Town
There are strangers
there are lovers
out on Fairfax in a line

They look me in the eye and say
"Our thoughts are intertwined."

And who am I
to doubt them?

And who are you
to tear down
these signs?

Midnight Strikes Too Soon

Cathy's hailing a cab
Like she's hailing a storm
Unto the streets of New York City.
Once we're inside, it's a carnival ride
that brings a white-knuckle kind
of dizzy.

She takes me up on her rooftop,
framed by a backdrop
of watertanks and chimneys.
She's wrapped 'round a cigarette,
lecturing etiquette, while I
look in the windows
beneath me.

We took in Saturday,
and it was medicine,
And when nighttime came the skyline
just swallowed
the moon.

Cathy lays the blame on Thomas Alva Edison
and 60 million lightbulbs telling New York that
it's noon.
Ah, midnight strikes too soon.
Midnight strikes too soon.

She says, "In New York City, they throw their
wishes into wells, 'cause you can't see a star,
unless one hit you when it fell—"
"And if even you caught one," I say, "Who
could you tell in this whole damn town, who'd
believe you?"

She smiled like a cat would to a pigeon on the roof.
She says, "I look into windows for universal truths,"
and we drank in the moment like
whiskey, hundred-proof.
"If Orion fell," she said, "I'd tell you."

The view from her roof could make your head
just spin.
It was like holding up the world in a tablespoon,
and we drank it down, every light in town,
like the sweetest, kindest medicine.
I made my wish on a satellite dish,
but still midnight strikes too soon.
Midnight strikes too soon.

Cathy never seems to slow down;
she's a hurricane working a skyscraper town.
She laughs at me, says I'm suburban bound,
but the truth is I live on a highway.

I come to this city for the solace of her roof.
Every window tells a story in cold hard truth.
As the world spins beneath me, I ask it for proof
that I'm living my life in my own way
or will time just have its own say.

Midnight strikes too soon
Midnight strikes too soon
Midnight strikes too soon
Midnight strikes too soon

The World Ain't Slowin' Down

I found you sittin'
On a suitcase cryin'.
Beneath my feet, I feel
The rumble of a subway train.
I laugh outloud.
'Cause it's the one thing
I hadn't been tryin'.
The train came in breathless,
You looked at me restless and said,
"Baby, you'll never change…"

You gotta get gone,
You gotta get goin'.
Hey, the world ain't slowin' down for no one.
It's a carnival calling out to you.

It sounds like a song;
It hits you like scripture.
You paint the picture
With colors squeezed from your hand.

Weren't you the kid
Who just climbed on the merry go round?
Hey look—the world ain't slowin down.

Out on the sidewalk,
Pigeons do the moonwalk.
Me, I'm dancing
Like Fred Astaire.
The lamp posts are rockin',
The whole town's talkin'
Like a fool
In a barber's chair.

I get the sensation, joy and frustration,
Like being caught by a drop of cold rain.
Freedom can numb you when there's no place to run to.
It feels just like novocaine.

You packed up all your handbags;
You're throwing off the sand bags;
I let go when you stepped free.

I didn't want to lose you. You said, "You didn't choose to—
It's just how your karma came."

Thanks for the vision, and the twenty-twenty wisdom.
It hit me like a south-bound train.

ACKNOWLEDGEMENTS

Lisa Murdock, for her arduous labors
of journal-mining, thank you.

Dave Perry at Sing/Song Books,
for thoughtful design
and inspirational insight.

Kirsten Carle, for assistance
and editing of the above.

Lisa Fehl-Parrette, for guidance in work and in life.

Ralph Jaccodine, for 10 years of friendship,
hard work, and daydreaming.

Sharon Teeler, for the cover photo,
and for a lifetime
of what will be.

Liz Linder for the head shot.

Rounder Records, Fleming/Tamulevich, Fan Out,
SESAC, and The Farrelly Brothers

And most importantly,
to all the friends and family who
appear in these songs and stories—
thanks for being there
to inform my words
and thoughts.

The lyrics presented herein
were taken from these fine albums:

Urban Folk Songs
Am I Home
Say Something
Stories
A Carnival of Voices
Translucent Soul
Live
Sweet Mistakes

For more information
about Ellis Paul's
music, writing and artwork,
please visit
www.ellispaul.com,
or write to the nice folks at:

Black Wolf Press
PO Box 381982
Cambridge, MA 02238

and they will be happy to give you
all of the details.